# Both Sides of the Desk

First published in the United States by
Old Baldy Press
Rochester, New York

Copyright © 2009
Robert Kinsella and Janine DeBaise

First Printing 2009

ISBN 978-0-9761157-2-4 (Paperback)
ISBN 978-0-9761157-3-1 (Electronic book)
LCCN 2008908382

All rights reserved. No part of this publication may be reproduced or transmitted in any form, or by any means, without the prior permission of the author.

# Contents

Dedication .................................................................... i
Introduction ................................................................ iii
Song, Dance, and Memories .......................................... 1
First Day Chaos ............................................................ 13
Hamburger Art ............................................................. 26
Behind Closed Doors .................................................... 40
Goblin Parade ............................................................... 53
She's a Honey ............................................................... 67
Death of a Teacher ........................................................ 83
A Peek Inside the Principal's Office ............................ 106
Snow Flakes and Sleigh Bells ..................................... 128
Flunking Out .............................................................. 140
Learning to Teach ....................................................... 160
Measuring Kids ........................................................... 172
Hearts, Flowers and Melted Ice Cream ...................... 184
Flag at Half Mast ........................................................ 193
Big Yellow Bus Ride ................................................... 209

## Dedication

*Jimmy DeMarco lived only nine years, from 1959 to 1968. He had an advanced case of Cystic Fibrosis. Many people at that time believed that handicapped children belonged at home or in a special class. Jimmy proved that being in a regular school was not only good for him but also enriched the lives of the other children. All who knew him will always treasure the memory of this smiling, happy child with his inquisitive mind and his love for people.*

*In Jimmy DeMarco's memory all profits from the sale of this book will go to the Cystic Fibrosis Foundation.*

## Introduction

The parents of today's school-age children may find it hard to remember a time when schools were a safe place for their children. Local newspapers are filled with the kind of horror stories that would make any parent worry. Schools today have metal detectors, security staffs, and a police presence.

But there was a time not long ago, when things were different. From 1966 to 1985, Bob was principal of an elementary school in Central New York. This book came from stories he collected during that time. The stories are true, but we've changed some of the names. And for the sake of simplicity, some of the characters are composites. Janine, his co-author, entered kindergarten in 1966 in the same school district. Her memories blend with Bob's experience to show an elementary school from both sides of the desk.

# Chapter 1
# Song, Dance, and Memories

It was 1984. In the high school library, we were working fast to set up video equipment. The announcement had just gone over the PA system, and kids were already trickling into the room. Juniors and seniors, these kids had been the cast for an elementary school play seven years earlier. We had gathered them to watch the play one last time – and to talk about their elementary school experiences. The kids looked kind of bored as they sauntered in, most were seniors after all and this was late afternoon on a hot June day, but their faces brightened as they recognized their old principal. And when they realized we had a tape of the old play, we were greeted with squeals of excitement and big grins.

Bob was about to retire, after twenty years as principal of Minoa Elementary, a small town elementary school in Central New York. Janine, thirty years younger, had gone through that school system as a student and graduated from college with a degree in creative writing. Bob had raised six kids, and Janine would raise four.

Janine's first job out of college was teaching computer programming to elementary school kids – and Bob was the one who hired her. This work relationship led to a friendship that included many discussions – and sometimes arguments – about elementary education. Janine taught as a secondary school teacher and then later taught writing and literature at the college level, but she had strong opinions about elementary education. As she raised her own kids and talked about parenting with other young parents, she often found herself retelling the many stories Bob told her about the children he had worked with during his twenty years as principal.

That's how this book came to be. Janine's memories of school as a student and Bob's stories about the students he had when he was principal are blended together. This book is collaboration between grandfather and feminist, between principal and teacher, between veteran and liberal, between two friends who like to read and argue – and who care about children.

On the afternoon of that hot June day, we were just beginning to write the book. Bob had been telling Janine stories about a great elementary school music teacher whose students perform the play "Electric Sunshine Man." When he remembered that he had a video of the play, we realized this was an opportunity to learn about an elementary school from the other side of the desk. That's how we ended up over at the local high school getting together an impromptu reunion of the original cast.

Bob explained to the students that he had gathered them together to see the video of their play, "The Electric Sunshine Man." What had been a roomful of bored teenagers barely acknowledging

## Song, Dance, and Memories

each other was transformed instantly into one group of excited kids laughing and talking as they crowded up to the television. They were surprised but excited to watch the videotape of the play they performed seven years ago.

"We're really going to watch the play?"
"You kept that tape!"
"It was so long ago!"
"I can't believe this!"
"I'm going to be embarrassed!"

The music began and the camera panned the stage.

"My gosh--the stage looks so little!"
Heads nodded in agreement.
"It seemed so huge when we were on it."
The music teacher appeared on the screen, directing the chorus.
"Look! There she is!"

The girls were all squealing with excitement at the sight of their former teacher. Susan--having dropped her purse, her books, and her snobbish attitude--exchanged smiles with the girls around her. "I miss her."

The music stopped, and the play began. The teenagers were all quiet now; their eyes fixed on the screen.

Michelle sat in the front row, with her elbows on an empty chair and her head between her hands. She stared at the screen, never moving as she watched herself dance across the stage with the other girls. She started to tap her feet to the music.

## Both Sides of the Desk

She had been tall for her age in fifth grade, a cute girl with a little button nose. She was still tall and slim, but her pretty face had taken on the strained, tired look of an older girl. As he looked at her, Bob remembered his conversation with John, the high school principal. They were discussing the students in the play, and as usual, he was kidding Bob about how bad his ex-students were. Bob told him that they were great kids until they came under his influence.

Michelle's name came up. "What a neat kid she was!" Bob remembered aloud. "She was one of the best dancers--so full of energy."

John turned to him, and his smile was gone. In a quiet voice, he told him about Michelle. Every weekend and many school nights, she was going to the local bars, dancing with anyone who would buy her a drink. By the end of the night she'd be smashed and would let anyone take her home. As a freshman she was an honor student--now, she was barely passing. "She used to be a super kid, popular, lots of friends," said John. "Now all the kids make fun of her."

"John, isn't there anything you can do for her?"

"We tried to get her help but her mother insists that we are imagining things--she won't let us do anything for her."

"What a shame."

"She could be one of our top students."

## Song, Dance, and Memories

Michelle's laugh, as one of the young actors kept stumbling over the word *simultaneously* brought Bob's mind back to the play.

"That was a big word in those days!" the teenager said defending himself.

When the first dance scene came up, John, the boy who played Thomas Edison, groaned. "Oh no! I remember how terrible I was at dancing."

"You kept crossing over with the wrong foot, remember?"

"It's like you're in slow motion--like the six-million-dollar man."

"Here's where you trip, John!"

Matt and Scott were sitting together. They turned to kid with John. What an unlikely pair they made--the scholar and the troublemaker. It's probably the first they had talked to each other in seven years.

As John finished singing his number, another student turned and said, "John, you were good!"

Lisa immediately popped up, "John, you weren't just good--you were great!"

Lisa was a beautiful girl with jet-black hair, probably one of the most popular girls in school. As John looked at her, it was obvious her compliment had made his day.

On the screen, a rigged-up light bulb in center stage suddenly went on.

"Look!" exclaimed the youngsters on stage, and their teenage counterparts watching the tape finished the line with them: "It's glowing!"

"You never forget the lines," said John.

"I still have the script at home," Karen admitted.

By now, many of the teenagers were reciting lines along with the youngsters on the tape. When one young actor hesitated, groping for a forgotten word, the teenagers all chimed in at once: "Bamboo." The youngster on stage repeated it after them: "Bamboo!"

"You only had four lines, and you forgot one," someone teased the teenaged Scott.

"It wasn't my fault. I didn't even know what bamboo was."

"We all knew everyone's lines. If someone slipped, we all would jump in."

"Remember how nervous we were in the dressing room?"

"Weren't we silly?"

"Wasn't it wonderful?"

Even after the tape was over, the group stayed--all jammed in the corner by the television screen, laughing and remembering.

"What happened to Miss Darnell?" they all wanted to know. "Did she ever get married? Does she have any kids?"

Gloria Darnell, the music teacher they so loved, never did marry. She was still teaching, although in another school district. Our attendance

## Song, Dance, and Memories

had dropped and she was the last music teacher hired--so with the policy of all the school districts, she was the first fired. With her departure went the musical. No other music teacher would dedicate so much time to the children.

Bob talked to her after she started at her new school. There were 300 kids in the school where she now was teaching and last year 232 had signed up for chorus. She was, of course, as popular with the kids as ever.

The fourth period bell rang and the group of teenagers broke up reluctantly, each student headed towards a different classroom.

John, the boy who had played Thomas Edison, spoke to me shyly. "Thanks, Mr. Kinsella. This was great. I haven't seen most of these kids in years." He motioned to the others, teenagers he probably at least passed in the halls every day. "None of us hang out together--different classes and stuff. It was just the play that brought us together."

"Just the play," Bob echoed his words softly.

"None of us will ever forget it," John said.

That elementary school play, an event that led to such treasured memories for these kids, began with Gloria Darnell, a gifted music teacher who worked with Bob in the early 1980s. Gloria loved music and children and she knew how to get the school excited about her projects. After Christmas vacation, pictures of Thomas Edison and his many inventions appeared on the bulletin board. Across the top she had written in big black letters: "Who is this Man?" Under the pictures were the words, "Ask your teacher or look in the library for more information. In May this man will change Minoa Elementary School." The children all looked curiously at the posters as they passed to their class. Gloria had talked last spring about the great musical she would put on next year. Fourth and fifth grade teachers knew, upon seeing the bulletin board, that Gloria wanted them to teach the children about Thomas Edison. Most willingly cooperated, knowing that the children would be eager to learn.

Soon, a new poster that read "The Electric Sunshine Man" replaced the Thomas Edison poster. In smaller print it said: "A Musical about Thomas Edison will be put on in the Minoa Elementary Music Hall (Cafeteria) on May 28th & 29th. Actors from Minoa Elementary School will star in this new production."

It was still only early February and Gloria had begun to get the children excited about the May performance. Later, Gloria put a large sheet of poster board on a wooden easel to the side of the latest signs she hung for "The Electric Sunshine Man." The new sign had an arrow pointing to the cafeteria and read: "Tryouts for the musical 'The Electric Sunshine Man' begin Monday."

Teachers wondered how many kids would give up recess to learn about the musical and the tryout process. The answer was: almost all of them.  The bigger mystery to all of us was wondering how Gloria was ever going to select a cast. She hated being selective. Every year when she was holding tryouts for her chorus, she would announce that she was going to take only the good singers, but no one believed her. She hated to turn any child away. By the time she began talking to the children about joining chorus her requirements dropped to any child who wanted to sing.

Gloria solved the problem by choosing a play that had lots of small parts. And any child who did not want to sing or dance was recruited to help build sets. Pretty soon almost every child in fourth and fifth grade was involved, and every child was made to feel that his role was important. Even pulling the curtain became an important job.

By mid-April the topic of conversation in Minoa Elementary was the musical. The auditions had taken place in early March and the chorus had been practicing songs since January. The final cast for the play had studiously memorized their lines for the first rehearsal in April. Gloria had recruited mothers over Christmas to help with all the sewing for the costumes and sets. A team of young student artists worked with the art teacher, painting the backdrops. In a move that surprised everyone, Donny, the tough, swaggering bully of the fifth grade, was recruited to supervise the painting crew in February. But Gloria knew what she was doing. Donny rose to the occasion, directed the kids in a quiet but forceful way, and the backdrops were sensational.

By April the cast was practicing every night with Gloria manipulating faculty and parents to give the kids rides home. Her resourcefulness was amazing. The planning and preparation needed to produce a successful musical was staggering. But she confronted each challenge with her usual good nature and energy--and somehow everything was done.

Every fourth and fifth grader was excitedly looking forward to the big day in May. No member of the cast would consider missing a rehearsal and school attendance during April was at record levels.

One story Bob tells comes from a day on the playground watching the children. The warm weather had brought the return of playing outside during lunch hour and the activity and laughter was fun to watch. He listened to a group of children climbing and hanging from the jungle gym. They were talking about the musical.

"Wait 'till you see the backdrop for the scene in the invention factory," said one of the children. He was one of the young artists recruited by Gloria.

"Yeah. We painted hundreds, no, thousands of bottles," another boy said. "Wait 'till you see it."

Walking to the bleachers by the baseball field Bob overheard the conversation of a group of girls on the swing set. "We went extra late with rehearsals last night," Lisa, a fifth grader, told her

## Song, Dance, and Memories

friends. "We do everything over and over. It has to be just perfect."

The members of the cast seemed to assume an importance they'd never had before. Lisa was a ditch digger in the musical laying the electric cables. She didn't have a single line.

Gloria often would join the kids on the playground as soon as she was done with lunch. She always injected excitement in the children and everyone wanted to talk to her.

In May the big day finally arrived. There were two shows during the day for the younger grades and one at night for the community. The mothers, who had patiently sewed the costumes, took over the stage makeup. The props came from everywhere, including a chair from Bob's living room.

For the night show, the cafeteria was crowded with parents, siblings, and younger students--many of whom had already seen the show at least once. The nervous young actors and actresses in costumes and makeup kept darting through the crowd on countless important errands. The chorus milled about on the bleachers.

Bob Jubinville, who was in charge of the video equipment in another school district, loaned us the spotlights for the show. We sent a special invitation to him so that he could see the production.

For the grand finale the cast streamed onto the stage, dancing and singing with arms outstretched and huge smiles on their faces as the chorus sang, "Nothing is impossible." The cast kicked legs in unison in a chorus line, arms about each other's shoulders. Gloria motioned to the singers in the bleachers and they repeated the refrain of the song one last time. No one wanted it to end.

Mr. Jubinville, after the show, said, "That was truly a professional performance. It's the best kids' show I ever saw." He hesitated and then asked, "Would you let me tape it for our local television station?"

Gloria was thrilled and they scheduled the performance for the following week.

The taping of the performance went beautifully and the children who performed were thrilled to see themselves on television. That was the tape we brought back to show those same kids, seven years later.

## Chapter 2
## First Day Chaos

Most adults remember their own first day of school but few have witnessed the opening of school from the principal's perspective, the chaos behind the scenes. Every year, the first few days of school are controlled turmoil. Teachers are preparing for students they have never met and children are concerned about what their teacher will be like. Both teachers and students say they hate to see the summer end – and yet when those yellow buses pull up to the school, you can feel the excitement in the air. The curving walk and green lawn that had been quiet all summer rings with the shouts and laughter of children as the buses unload students.

For a principal, the new year begins when teachers begin appearing in late summer preparing their classrooms for their new students. The beige rooms that look so clean but impersonal disappear beneath a rainbow of colors, each room taking on the personality of the teacher. Dorothy, a veteran kindergarten teacher, was always the first person back. She'd spend days lugging in plants, pieces of carpet, and all kinds of books and games for the learning centers she'd set up all over her room. Some teachers carefully labeled the desks so that shy kids would know where to sit.

## Both Sides of the Desk

Janine remembers how important it was to have the desks labeled. A shy kid, she was always terrified on the first day of school. Her bus was often the last one to the school, and by the time she would enter the classroom, the seats near the front of the room would be taken, and she would have to sit near some of the loud boys. When her youngest child, a shy kid like herself, began school, he had a wonderful kindergarten teacher who encouraged the kids to stop by the school the week before it opened. When she came in with her son, the teacher showed him his desk, carefully and colorfully labeled with his name, and told him that is where he would sit on the first day. She could see how relieved he was to know this.

Unfortunately, not every teacher understood or cared about making the children feel welcome. Norma, a fourth grade teacher, wouldn't appear until the morning school began. She'd pull out the same pictures and posters she used every year and stick them up quickly, probably using the same tacks and holes she used the year before. Then she would rush to the teacher's room for coffee and gossip.

The challenge for Bob on the first day of school was remembering all the children's names. The boys often looked the same--just taller and tanned. But the girls seemed to change the most. The little girl with the long brown braids might now have a head full of curls, bleached by the summer sun. Then sometimes a child might fool him by

## First Day Chaos

looking exactly like an older brother or sister two Septembers ago.

The newest students, the kindergarteners, always moved slowly, climbing out of the buses with looks of bewilderment. Their paper identification tags, pinned on by anxious parents at home, seemed huge on such tiny bodies. Some of the little ones bubbled with chatter and smiles, but others were wide-eyed and silent, gazing at the teachers solemnly. Every year, of course, we'd get a crying child, a little one who simply did not want to come to school.

Usually Bob would see a mother, looking worn out, dragging her kindergarten child toward school. Between the sobs, the kid would be begging, "Mom, please don't make me go to school! I promise, I'll go tomorrow." Experienced teachers knew how to handle this. A teacher like Gloria would calmly disentangle the child from his mother, "He'll be fine," she would say firmly to the mother. "I promise that he'll be fine as soon as he gets into the classroom." Then she would walk the child to his classroom.

The child would continue screaming and kicking and yelling that he didn't want to go to school even as he entered his classroom. But within minutes, once he realized his parent was gone, he'd calm down and maybe even play with some toys. Often recognizing another child in the room was enough.

Janine remembers her own first day of kindergarten. Her parents had prepared her carefully, sending her in the June before with her sister to spend the day in kindergarten. She loved cutting things out of construction paper and using as much glue as she wanted. Her parents were probably surprised then, on the first day of school, when she ran screaming from the bus, refusing to get on until her father carried her on and deposited her in the front seat.

The big challenge was getting the children home on the right buses. There were countless incidents of children forgetting their bus numbers and little kids upset because they were afraid they wouldn't make it home to their parents. Janine can remember worrying about missing her bus: from lunchtime on, she would look nervously at the clock. Somehow a shy child gets the idea that if she misses the bus, she will be doomed to spend the rest of her life wandering the lonely halls of an empty school.

To help eliminate confusion with the buses, Bob asked every teacher without a homeroom to greet the children as they arrived. Each teacher had a stack of slips with bus numbers written on them. As each bus pulled up, a teacher would hand every single child on the bus a slip of paper that had on it the number of the bus he arrived on and the number of the bus he would be taking home. They gave the slip to their classroom teacher who recorded it so that she knew the number of the bus they were to take home. The system ended many problems but not all. By the time Bob would get back to his office, his secretary Alice would have a list of messages waiting for him:

*Jimmy's Mom drove him to school. He doesn't know what bus he rides.*

*Karen is crying. She walked to school and forgot her bus number.*

*Bobby is going to a baby sitter and didn't know where she lives.*

So on the first day, Bob spent the morning making phone calls, checking bus schedules, and visiting every classroom to verify that every child knew what bus to take home. He knew how terrified kids would be if they ended up on the wrong bus or if they missed the bus altogether.

Making the rounds gave Bob a chance to check in with each teacher. He recalls the time that Sam, a fifth grade teacher, was concerned about Andrea, a student in his class. She and her little brother were to be dropped off at her grandmother's. When she handed him the note, she said, "My mother ran away this summer, you know."

The tragedies that happened in the lives of some of these kids, revealed often by a very casual remark, were frightening. It was frustrating to know there was little a teacher or principal could do. To confirm she knew her bus number, Bob checked with her in the gym. Andrea produced the note from her father; she knew the correct bus to take to get to her grandmother's. She gave him the information with no trace of emotion in her voice, and sitting down again crossed her legs and started talking to a girl next to her. It was amazing how resilient a fifth grader can be, or at least appear to be.

Back in the office, the principal's secretary Alice would be taking calls from worried parents, getting intercom messages from concerned teachers, and soothing crying children. She would sometimes stop Bob to look at a note she had gotten from a parent. For instance, one time she showed him a note from a family who had recently moved away. The message here was brief: "To Minoa Elementary, would you please send transfers for my three children, to destination unknown."

Mid-morning the first grade teachers led their first graders to the cafeteria. This would be the first day they could buy milk or lunch, and the teachers were letting them have a practice round. Solemnly, the children would march up to the counter, one by one, and pretended to hand the cafeteria woman some money. She smilingly accepted each little fistful of air and handed the child two graham crackers. On this first day, the children were quiet and shy. They sat at the tables munching the crackers and not even saying a word.

The three large yellow buses always arrived early for our morning kindergarten children. It was a relief to see them waiting with open doors and engines running. Each child had a large white tag with his name and bus number on it, but from experience, we knew when the first bus number was called, every single child would get up to leave. They were terrified of missing their bus. Janine well remembers this feeling: on the first day of school, she would start getting nervous as soon as she came back from lunch. The thought of not getting the right bus home is a shy child's worst nightmare.

All of the extra staff -- music, art, gym, speech, reading, and library -- were on hand to help the children onto the buses. They would lead groups of youngsters to the bus -- hugging the frightened ones, joking with the shy ones, and sometimes even heading right on the bus to introduce them to the driver.

Bob always breathed a sigh of relief when the last buses left. It was quiet for a moment but he knew that soon they would be deluged with calls from worried parents, nervous that their children weren't home from school on time. The buses were frequently late the first few days -- the drivers and the children were still learning the route. Other children, seeing their friends get off, would begin to cry, sure every time the driver stopped it was their house. One year a boy was most convincing when he pointed to a house and yelled, "That's my house!" The bus driver laughed. It was his house and he said, "And he sure wasn't my kid."

One little boy when asked his bus number confidently said, "One two three four." The teacher looked at her sheet and then back at him. "Tommy,

I don't think that's right." He tried again: "five six seven eight?"

Of course just getting the students on the bus did not guarantee the children would get home. Sometimes a bus driver would return with a crying child and often all he had was a first name. Danny was one of these children. The only thing he would tell the bus driver is that he lived in a white house. Every time he asked him his last name, he would just clamps his lips tighter together. Finally, the driver brought him back to school so that a teacher could come up with his name and address.

Thirty minutes late, the driver arrived at Danny's house. His mother and father were both waiting as Danny got off crying. Danny's father, frightened and angry, turned to the driver and yelled, "Look what you did to my son. Why don't you learn your route?"

Later the driver told Bob what the father said. He shook his head. "It was a brown house, Bob."

Many of the younger children would be tired after their first full day back. The first-graders, especially, had to adjust to the longer day. A first grade teacher told Bob once that she had a little boy who found his first day so incredibly long that he thought dismissal would never come. At lunchtime he asked eagerly when he could go home. During their first spelling lesson he asked again--wasn't it time to leave? Finally in mid-afternoon, he asked in

## First Day Chaos

a worried tone, "Will it still be daylight when we go home?"

Bus problems are expected but other school happenings occur in those first days that are surprising, embarrassing, sad, and even frightening.

Some lively kindergarten kids just can't stay in the classroom. They want to go home. It was a common problem but, until Dennis, we never had one actually escape. Bob can remember getting a worried intercom message from Dennis' teacher. Dennis, a brown-haired little boy was quietly trying to slip out of the room. Bob hurried down to the room to talk to the little boy.

Kneeling down to be at his eye level, Bob asked, "What's the matter Dennis?" The child looked at the floor and didn't say a word. "Where are you going?"

"I'm going home," he muttered.

"Dennis, I feel bad that you don't like our school. Your teacher will be hurt if you leave. She planned a nice song for you to sing and has paper for you to draw on. She'll miss you."

Bob raised his voice and spoke to the teacher: "Mrs. Cisternino, I am going to lock your door."

The teacher nodded. She knew that the door couldn't be locked on the inside, but Dennis wouldn't know this. Bob closed the door and crouched down behind it, trying to hold the doorknob without being seen. Sure enough, in a few minutes, he felt the pressure of a little hand

trying to turn the knob. Bob held it fast. What he didn't notice was the little face peering up at him through the mail slot. After a few moments, he let go of the knob and returned to his desk. A short time later, he got a frantic call from the teacher,
"Bob, I can't find Dennis."
"He's not in the classroom?"
"I think he's started home. He lives over on the main drag."

Bob borrowed Alice's car. Quickly driving down the main street, he spotted Dennis. The little guy was walking determinedly at the side of the road. When he saw the principal behind him, he started running.

Bob threw the car into park, yanked the keys from the transmission, and began chasing Dennis on foot. The tiny boy darted across the road with the principal in hot pursuit. Just as he was to grab the child, Dennis turned and ran the other way. Bob turned too--or at least he tried to. In slippery, leather-soled dress shoes, his feet wouldn't obey him. He skidded helplessly in the wrong direction.

The little boy had no trouble at all negotiating turns in his well-worn sneakers. Bob's legs were twice as long as his, yet he couldn't keep up. Those leather-soled shoes skidded every time, and at every turn he slid merrily in the wrong direction. Back and forth they went, across that smooth-paved road. Breathing heavily by now, wondering how long he could take this, knowing

*First Day Chaos*

the chances of ever getting back to school before the buses arrived seemed slim.

In the midst of this crazy dashing back and forth, Bob became aware of a spectator. Chuck Lorraine, a neighbor with three kids in the school, had paused out on his lawn where he had been raking leaves and stood, hands on rake, watching Bob lose a race to a five-year-old. Bob's face grew red as he listened to his good-natured chuckles. After what seemed like an eternity, he finally grabbed Dennis's shirt.

"Come on," he tried to speak gently but the anger must have been obvious. He helped the child into the car, carefully buckling the seatbelt. "Your teacher wants you back in the classroom, and you can draw a picture to bring home to your mother. Won't that be nice?"

Chuck flashed a V for victory sign and gave them a big wave good-bye. Bob decided he would never again go alone to chase a child. And he vowed never to wear leather-soled shoes to school.

The end of the first day was always just as hectic. Crazy stuff happened right up to the end of the day. One year, Bob was just about to make the announcement to dismiss students when the door to the office lobby burst open and a mother raced in.

"Can you excuse Davy, Rob, and Cindy?" she began, "I'm taking them to the dentist." Mrs. Damm was an active member of the PTO. She stood before him in a trench coat nervously rattling her car keys. "If they get on the bus, they'll miss their appointment."

Looking at the class list posted beside the PA system, Bob realized that he couldn't reach all three of her children without holding up the buses. Lifting the microphone to his mouth, he announced, "Please send all the Damm children to the office immediately."

The switchboard lit up immediately. One of the fourth grade teachers came on first: "Can I send all the damn kids down?"

Mrs. Damm, who was twirling her car keys with one hand, covered a smirk on her face with the other. Bob laughed and said, "I think we'll manage to get your kids down here shortly, or at least some damn kids."

Another time a parent called at the beginning of the second day and said that she had kept her son home from school. She was irate. She yelled, "You put my child in the Catholic school yesterday. I don't want him to go there again. I'm not even Catholic!"

"Are you sure?"

"I've never been Catholic!"

"No, I mean, how do you know he went to the Catholic school?"

"His teacher was Sister Nino."

There was a Catholic elementary school right across the road, but we'd never had a student go there by mistake. He was assigned to Pauline Cisternino and had been in her classroom the day

*First Day Chaos*

before, yet his mother insisted that his teacher was Sister Nino. Bob puzzled over this, but Alice smiled and said, "Bob, Pauline Cisternino is the Sister Nino."

The first day of school seems to be an eternity for staff and children, filled with all kinds of craziness. Every year we expect the unexpected. It's part of what makes elementary school teaching so wonderful.

## Chapter 3
## Hamburger Art

What happens in the cafeteria is as much a part of school life as what happens in the classroom. A visit to a school cafeteria can be very revealing. In schools where children fear punishment, the cafeteria can be an unpleasant place but in a school with a friendly, nurturing atmosphere, lunchtime can be a positive experience.

Classroom teachers dreaded lunch duty. They took turns monitoring the students during the lunch hour. Some teachers expected the cafeteria of over 200 children to be as quiet as their classrooms. It was trying and the duty made for a long day for these teachers. In some schools the teachers blew whistles or flick the light on and off for quiet—usually with little effect. Some teachers just screamed at the kids. Norma was one of these teachers. Sullen and obviously still angry at having cafeteria duty, she walked about the cafeteria yelling at the children as they ate. One time, she screamed at Donny, a frequent visitor to the office, and began to scold him. Donny picked up his tray and threw it across the room.

Seeing the principal come into the room, Donny jumped into the return tray window used by the children to drop off their trays when they had finished eating. Carol, the cafeteria supervisor was shocked to see a boy suddenly appear in her return tray window. Donny scrambled off the conveyer belt and kept going, down the cafeteria hallway and into the janitor's office and into the bathroom where he locked the door. When told to come out, he defiantly yelled, "Make me!" Larry, the janitor, took out a dime, put it in the groove on the doorknob, and opened it. A surprised and subdued Donny followed Bob quietly to the office.

The pressure of 600 children crowding through one lunch counter was frustrating, but had its funny and moving moments. Parents, fearful that the children would lose their lunch money, made them put their money deep in their pockets before they left home. When it came time to pay they often couldn't get their money out of their tight jeans. Carol would call Larry who sometimes had to lift the child off the floor so their pants would loosen and he or she could get at the money.

And then there were the children who would get to the cash register and panic because they couldn't find their money. Carol calmly told them to turn their pockets inside out--almost always solving the problem.

Sneakers caused a unique problem. A sneaker company marketed a sneaker with a pocket. Peter, a second grader, was the first of many kids to convince his parents to buy these sneakers. And like the other kids, it didn't take him long to decide the pocket was a good place to put his lunch money. When Peter got to the cash register, his first day with the new sneaks, he bent over to unzip the pocket, but he couldn't get it open. So Peter sat down on the floor, bringing the lunch line to a complete halt, took off his sneaker, and carefully unzipped the pocket and got his money. Then he stuck the sneaker back on his foot, and with shoelaces dangling, shuffled to a table. Unfortunately the sneaker-with-the-pocket was a fad that really caught on with the younger children. Carol threatened to sue the company for the aggravation it caused her.

Another common problem for the children was getting the right change. Occasionally it would all be in pennies--especially the day before mom or dad's payday.

The cafeteria staff at our school played an important role in setting a positive atmosphere. A hungry child found extra portions on his plate. A child without money would be given lunch and a charge slip. The women serving the lunches talked to the children as they came through the line, with jokes that got smiles from the shyest of them. Monday was hamburger day. The children usually took a little extra time at the condiment table to make faces on their hamburgers with the ketchup and mustard squeeze bottles. Carol, the cafeteria supervisor, was good-natured about the creative efforts of the children, but if the line began backing up, she'd laugh and shoo them over to their tables: "That's enough art work for today. Save some energy for art class!"

## Hamburger Art

The breakfast program, new to our school, was started so that all children would have a nutritious breakfast to start the day. While Minoa was generally a village of middle class families, many families had low enough income to qualify their children for a free or reduced breakfast according to the state's guidelines. Many, including administrators, teachers, and parents, thought the breakfast program was a waste of taxpayers' money.

If only they could see children like Mandy and Rick trudging to school every day to join their friends for breakfast. The two young children could be seen splashing through puddles, or plowing through snow, with Rick tugging at his sister's coat to hurry her along. Their dad was in jail for his third DWI. Their mother worked two jobs but both were minimum pay. Most of her pay went for rent and utilities. Opening the outside door one hour before the last bell gave her children not only breakfast but also a place to stay after she left for work.

Before the breakfast program many parents would drive around the circle, drop their children at the front door, and quickly drive away. Many hated dropping their kids off so early, but they had to leave for work before the school bus could get to their home. They had to decide to be late for work or have their children stay in the house alone, or worse, outside waiting for the bus. They were thrilled when they discovered that all children were welcome to attend the morning breakfast program. Some had to pay a nominal fee while for many it was free.

Carol, the cafeteria supervisor, monitored the children. She liked the idea of the children coming early. It gave her a chance to talk quietly with each of them. She knew that Bob was in his office and always available if needed. Intuitively she knew the best way to prevent problems was letting the children know she cared for each of them. She talked and joked with them. No one could miss her high-pitched laugh and rarely did she raise her voice.

The cafeteria staff were all mothers themselves, many of them with children in Minoa. They always took special steps to make the cafeteria pleasant. A problem that concerned the cafeteria staff was the children who forgot or didn't have lunch money. One first grade teacher's solution was to give children access to a jar in her desk filled with change. Kids who needed money took it out and then paid her back when they could. She did this for years without any problems.

Many other teachers sometimes gave money to their students for lunch, and most of them really couldn't afford to subsidize lunches. Yet, they never complained or let a child go without lunch. Eventually, the PTO started the lunch charge slip program. Charge slips were printed with room for a child's name, class and date. If a child forgot his lunch, the teacher filled out the charge slip, and the child gave the slip to the cafeteria cashier. The PTO fund paid the charges and when the child paid their teacher back they paid the charges. If a child forgot again before repaying, they would be issued another slip. If they forgot a third time, they were supposed to go without lunch. Carol, instead, had her staff make peanut butter and jelly sandwiches for these students. Surprisingly, children almost always paid their charge slips. It was rare that a child didn't pay after the first charge.

Bob often walked through the cafeteria at meal times. Lunchtime is an important time for the principal or teacher to observe the behavior of a child that they are worried about. Is the shy child making friends? Is the loud child learning to curb his own behavior? In fact, whenever a new child entered the school, we learned a great deal about the child just by observing where he sat. Quiet smart kids naturally gravitate towards other quiet smart kids. Kids who love sports sit with other athletes. The child who likes to get into mischief will find other kids who like to stir up trouble. A child having trouble in school might choose lunchtime to act out.

The cafeteria staff, who lived in the community and knew the families, were often able to alert Bob to problems with individual children. One time, for instance, Carol was surprised when Nancy, a fourth grader, tried to pay for lunch with a $20 bill. Carol knew Nancy's mother and was certain she would never give her a $20 bill. She gave Nancy her lunch but didn't take the money. She sent Bob a note instead.

When Nancy finished lunch, she was sent to the office. Bob asked if she had a $20 bill. Without a word, the little girl pulled the $20 bill from her pocket.

"Where did you get that?"

"From my friend Tammy."

"Tammy gave you $20?"

"I am holding it for her."

Nancy's blue eyes stared blankly from a freckled face. Bob sighed. This was going nowhere.

Bob then called Tammy to the office and asked if she had any money. She pulled a $20 bill from her dress pocket.

"Where did you get that?"

"From Nancy."

"Nancy gave you $20?"

"I am holding it for her."

Bob looked over at Nancy. Her face red, she looked down at her shoes.

Annoyed with their game playing, Bob took the two bills and put them on his desk, and said, "Nancy, this isn't your money." She nodded. "Tammy, this isn't your money." She nodded. Bob called in his secretary, Alice, who always knew enough to play along with his ideas.

"Alice, these two girls just found two $20 bill and have no idea who they belong to."

Alice said, "Maybe we can buy that new tape recorder we wanted."

Tammy with her arms crossed, stared at the floor. Nancy, her face pink between her red pigtails, was shifting uncomfortably from foot to foot and nudging her friend. Bob thanked the girls and told them to go back to class.

Right away, Bob called Nancy's mother.

"Are you by chance missing any money?" he asked.

"Yes," she said. "Forty dollars. My grocery money."

She was relieved that her money had been found, but upset of course that her daughter had taken it. She would be right over to get it.

Moments later, Nancy showed up in the principal's office.

"I lied," she said shyly. Bob felt relieved.

"It was the money my Gram and Gramp gave me for Christmas. I brought it to school without telling my Mom."

She looked up at me for the first time, her eyes pleading. "Please, don't call my Mom. She'd kill me."

Just then the intercom phone buzzed. Nancy's mother had arrived.

Nancy looked up when her mother walked in. Every freckle seemed to stand out on her pale, frightened face.

"Gram and Gramp gave me money for Christmas, remember?"

"Nancy," her mother said reproachfully, "Your grandparents gave you $5 and you only put $3 in your bank." She looked down at the floor, and for a moment, looked just like her daughter. Then she looked at me very quickly. "I am going to take Nancy home now. We have some talking to do."

They left the office, and that was the last Bob heard of the incident.

Another time, Carol asked Bob to come down to the breakfast program. "There is something I want you to see." Bob stood near her and watched while the bus children, who arrived later than the kids who walked, went through the line. Everything looked normal and Bob started to leave. Carol raised her one finger, gesturing that she wanted him to wait a little longer. The children in the cafeteria were quietly enjoying their breakfast when the last bell rang. Within minutes the cafeteria was empty as children left for their rooms. Then the sound of running feet broke the silence. Several fourth grade children rushed into line with coats still on and book bags in hand. They were eating as fast as they could as they passed through the line, and without breaking stride raced to their classroom with their cheeks still rosy from the cold outside air.

Bob knew immediately who their teacher was. Norma, a fourth grade teacher, thought the breakfast program was stupid. She kept children in from recess if they stopped for breakfast and were late for class. But a handful of her students were on a bus that consistently arrived late. They were so hungry they ate their breakfast as they passed through the line and then rushed to make it to class with the other students on their bus. "Those kids don't eat," Carol said, "They inhale their food."

During Bob's visits to the breakfast program, Bob noticed three girls who sat together every day, talking and laughing as they ate. They seemed to be close friends. On the playground they ignored each other. When asked why, one of the girls said, "Oh, they are just my morning friends."

Carol and Bob had a great working relationship, but he did one thing that drove her crazy. Faculty meetings were held in the cafeteria and often the noise from the freezer was annoying so he would turn it off, fully intending of course to turn it back on at the end of the meeting. One morning Carol stopped Bob in the hall with an annoyed look on her face and asked if he had had a faculty meeting the night before.

"Oh, no," Bob thought. He thought immediately of the freezer, which he had forgotten to turn back on. Visions of soupy ice cream came to his mind.

"Am I supposed to sell all this mushy, weird shaped ice cream?" Carol asked.

But she didn't let Bob suffer too long. Once she had had her joke, she explained that she had asked the custodian to double check the freezer after faculty meetings. She knew better than to trust Bob's memory.

No one was immune from Carol's humor, especially the custodian. Larry was a big shy man with a heart as big as his frame. One time, a tiny girl in first grade spilled a carton of milk on her dress. Without a word the girl pulled her dress off and handed it to Larry. He turned bright red and was trying not to even look at this little girl, dressed only in tights and an undershirt. He gently nudged the little girl over to Carol, and asked her to help. She just ignored him and his face got redder and redder. Then with a smile on her face she took the half dressed girl to Jane, our school nurse, who kept extra clothes in her office for just such emergencies.

Teachers often sent children to the office for misbehaving in the lunchroom. Donny was a frequent visitor. One time, he threw his lunch bag at another student. His excuse was that he didn't throw it far and besides Peter had been throwing peas at him the whole lunch time and he didn't get yelled at. He didn't think that was fair. This was typical, Donny trying to get other students into trouble. Bob knew that Peter was not the kind of kid to behave in that way. Usually Donny had better choices of students to blame.

Donny claimed that the reason the teacher didn't catch Peter was that he put the peas on his chair and flicked them up over the table so no one could see where they were coming from and that they were hitting his clean shirt. Bob decided to

## Hamburger Art

call his bluff. "Let's go to the cafeteria, and you can show me how he threw those peas at you."

With a smug expression on his face, convinced that Peter was in for a terrible punishment, Donny marched into the cafeteria. The cafeteria was empty and the staff was finishing cleaning the kitchen. Donny led his principal to the cafeteria table in the corner and pointed to a chair where he sat. Donny sat down in Peter's chair and the principal sat in Donny's chair. Carol put the bowl of cold peas requested on the table.

"Okay, " Bob said, "Put some peas on your chair and flick them at me the way Peter did."

"Sure," said Donny. He seemed excited at the prospect.

Carefully, he selected a handful of peas and set them on the edge of the chair. When the peas were in position, he looked up, smiled and with a flick of his forefinger and thumb he sent the first pea flying, landing under the table. The pea didn't even come near the principal. Still confident Donny brushed the hair out of his eyes and rearranged the remaining peas. With his right hand he reached down and flicked the second pea. This one sailed straight up, almost to the level of the table, before falling to the floor beside the chair. His chair, of course.

So Donny decided that Peter's chair had been pulled out a little. He rearranged the chair, pulling it away from the table at an unlikely angle. Concentrating now, his brow wrinkled in seriousness, he leaned over to flick another pea. This one went sideways and up, then fell down a foot from his chair. The next pea flew a bit further but didn't come close to the other side of the table. He moved the chair aside for his next attempt. A muffled choking sound was heard as Carol tried to contain her laughter. Bob didn't dare look up at the other doorway where he knew Alice was watching. One look at her and he knew he would burst into laughter.

    Donny was kneeling on the floor now and had the chair pulled out from the table. Around him peas were scattered in every direction, but despite all his efforts, not a single pea had made it up over the table. Donny was beginning to realize a pea would have to almost defy gravity to fly over the table.

    Still determined, he tried to flick yet another pea, and then another. Bob was beginning to wonder when his stubbornness would give out, and mentally cursed Carol for giving such a generous plateful of peas. Carol, of course, was enjoying the scene from the kitchen, and was probably ready to bring out another bowl.

    With a flick, Donny sent one pea into the table and it bounced back to hit him in the knee. Finally, Donny flopped back into the chair and folded his arms, "I don't know how he did it," he said, with one last spark of defiance. "But he did it."

*Hamburger Art*

All hopes of getting Peter in trouble had vanished. He quickly agreed to help clean the cafeteria with the custodian as his punishment.

Carol was good-natured about the whole incident.

"Thanks for your help," Bob said to her.

"No problem," she said, "This is great entertainment. Better than television."

## Chapter 4
## Behind Closed Doors

School bathrooms have always been a place for problems. This is where many kids have their first smoke. In the bathroom, away from the eyes of the teachers, even honor students act up and of course it is the place where problem children hatch their plans of revenge. Mid-October, for instance, the janitor would appear in Bob's office complaining that kids in the fifth grade boys' bathroom had been throwing wet paper wads onto the white ceiling. It was a quite harmless prank-- there was no real damage. But it was a nuisance to scrape the wads off the ceiling.

Bob kept notes on the problems that occurred in his school, and his notes showed that the wet paper wads were an annual event almost always occurring in mid-October. The culprits were not, as you might think, the usual mischief-makers but rather honor students, the good kids who had gotten tired of being teased as being teacher's pets, and needed to act out.

It is usually difficult to catch the kids responsible for problems in the bathroom but knowing the type of children simplified the problem. Armed with the clue that the culprits were probably "good kids" gave Bob an idea of how to solve the problem. He called on the help of one of the school troublemakers: a little boy named Donny.

Bob liked Donny and felt that deep down inside he was really a good kid. He had to live up to his reputation as a tough guy. He would be thrilled to perform a special mission for the principal--especially if it gave him a chance to get some of his least favorite classmates in trouble. So Bob send a note to his teacher and asked Donny to come down to the office. "Tell him he's not in trouble."

Donny swaggered into the office. He plopped himself down on one of the chairs. He was very familiar with the office; his mischievous mind had gotten him into trouble again and again over the past few years. Bob asked him if he notice that the ceiling in the boys' bathroom was getting plastered with wet paper wads.

"I didn't do it, Mr. Kinsella," he interrupted. "Honest." His dark brown eyes stared innocently and worried. Donny had enough trouble with the things he did do. It must have been more than he could bear to think he was now getting blamed for things he didn't do.

"Don't worry," Bob said, "I know that you aren't the one doing it. But it's a real problem for our custodian. Do you know who is doing it?"

A change rapidly spread over the boy's face. Donny the Falsely Accused quickly became Donny the Secret Informant.

"I can find out," he said.

"I would appreciate that," Bob said, "But please, just give me their names. Don't talk to them yourself." He knew that without this comment, Donny was likely to punch the kids in the mouth and claim the principal had told him to do so.

Two days passed and the ceiling of the bathroom continued to get peppered with wet paper wads.

Then Donny appeared in the principal's office. He took a seat and announced, "I been watching the lav."

Bob knew that was an understatement. He had probably lived in the lav the last two days. Donny reached into his pocket and pulled out a wrinkled paper with a list of names on it. He folded it carefully and gave it to his principal with an air of great importance. He had seen each of these kids shoot a spitball and was shocked at their behavior. For a moment a halo seemed to appear over his head.

Bob decided it might not be wise to open the list in front of Donny. He thanked him and just told him he would take care of it. With a big grin, Donny left the room, probably making another stop in the lav to make one last check before going back to his classroom.

The smudged piece of paper contained seven names. Just as expected they were seven "good kids." Bob decided to wait until after lunch before calling them down to the office so that it wouldn't destroy their entire day. During the lunch hour teachers were given the names of the fifth-grade students he needed to see. They were good students and the teachers probably thought they were getting some award. When lunch was over the seven boys were chatting in the outer office, joking around while they waited.

"Just sit here quietly. Don't say another word." Bob's stern voice and appearance surprised them. The grins faded and they looked at each other uncomfortably. Bob called Johnny in, choosing to deal with them one at a time. As Johnny walked obediently into the office, he took a quick glance at the other six frightened faces. They knew they had been caught.

Johnny, entering the office, began to sit down, but Bob stopped him with a stern serious voice.

"You can stand. This won't take long."

"Did you shoot wet paper wads on the ceiling?"

"Mr. Kinsella, I'm not the only one. Jerry, Billy, Rob. . . they did it too."

"Question. Did you do it?"

"Yes, Mr. Kinsella. I'm sorry, I'll never do it again. I swear I'll never do it again."

"Go outside, sit down, tell Jerry to come in, and don't say another word."

By the time the seventh child left, five new names were added to the list. Each of these students was called to the office to join the other seven. They readily admitted, they too had been shooting wet paper wads. All twelve scared boys were called into the office. Some stared at the floor, others at the desk. It was obvious they expected the police to arrive any second and haul them off to jail.

"Boys," Bob said, "What you did created a lot of extra work for our custodian. It has to stop."

The boys promised him that the behavior would stop. And he knew he could trust them. The problem was over for another year.

Girls' bathrooms weren't free of problems either. Graffiti was a way girls sometimes got attention. Often we would find notes written on the walls. Sometimes the note was mean, and sometimes it was funny or clever.

One time for instance, the janitor showed Bob a mean message about a girl named Linda. The note was signed by Terri. Bob knew that Terri didn't write it. She was a troublemaker and an easy target, but would never be that foolish. Linda was an immediate suspect. From past incidents Bob knew that girls would write about themselves in mean ways to get sympathy from others when their friends were mad at them. In this case, the girls would rally around Linda, fighting to be able to sit next to Linda in the cafeteria or play with her outside.

Bob called Linda to the office.

"Did you write that mean note about yourself on the bathroom wall and sign Terri's name?" asked Bob.

"No. I wouldn't write on the bathroom wall." Linda sat straight in the chair, her back stiff and rigid. She had her hair in pigtails and wore a pretty dress decorated with pink flowers. She looked shocked that Bob would even think such a thing.

Bob looked into her eyes and told her that her handwriting and the writing on the wall were similar and he was thinking of having her mother come and look.

"Don't do that," she said. "Please, Mr. Kinsella." A tear rolled down her cheek. She blurted out that she did it but didn't know why. Bob told her that he knew why. "Your friends were mad at you and you knew they would feel sorry for you when they read those terrible things on the wall."

She nodded her head, "Yes."

"But what you did hurt Terri."

Bob called Terri down to the office and made Linda tell her the story. Almost in tears, Linda explained to the other girl what she had done. "I'm sorry, Terri," she said. "I won't ever do it again. I promise."

Terri was emotionless. Her expression hadn't changed from when she walked in the office. "Oh, forget it. The other kids don't like me anyway."

When Terri and Linda left my office they were talking like long-lost friends. It was good for Terri, but Bob knew this friendship would only last

## Both Sides of the Desk

a few days. He also knew that Terri would never tell anyone the real story.

Linda faced an even bigger problem shortly after that incident. Linda's mother called and she wanted her daughter moved back into fourth grade. "She is reading at a fourth grade level so that's where she belongs." Bob scheduled a meeting for the very next day.

Linda and her parents arrived early. Bob asked Linda to wait in the outer office, and she was told that she would be part of any decision but that he wanted to talk to her parents first. Linda's mother was angry that as principal, he just didn't move her daughter back a grade. The father, a short, well-built man with thick black hair and strong hands, was silent. His hands were on his lap and he hunched forward in his seat.

Bob talked to them calmly. He had talked to Linda's teacher and he did not recommend setting Linda back a grade. Linda was reading at a fourth grade level but her teacher was willing to give her extra help and would set up a home study program for them. She felt Linda would be crushed if she was moved from her friends.

Linda's mother stared back stonily.

Bob looked at her dad, who hadn't said a word, and asked him: "Do you want to move your child back to fourth grade?"

"No. And we're not going to. But that doesn't mean that we shouldn't do it in June. I'm just not moving my daughter into the same grade as her younger brother in the middle of the school year. If I have to do it in June, I'll send her to a private school."

Linda's mother jumped up and stormed out of the office. She grabbed her daughter by the arm and dragged her down the front walk. The father stood up and walked to the door. He turned and said, "Dolores loves Linda. But she also had a difficult time in school and doesn't want the same for her. Deep down inside she knows it's the wrong thing to do. She'll come around. She always does."

After hearing Linda's story from Bob, Janine was talking to some teachers at the elementary school her kids attended when she heard them talk about graffiti. The teachers were upset that someone had written nasty things on the wall in the girl's bathroom about a nice girl in their school. The principal heard them talking and said, "You will never guess who finally admitted to writing on the walls!"

Janine remembering Linda's story said, "I know who wrote them. It was the nice girl the nasty note was about."

The principal looked at her in amazement: "How did you know?"

Even the youngest children in school created problems in the bathrooms. One time a first grader was caught piddling and throwing dirty paper in the wastebasket. The teacher caught him and sent him to the office with a note. He admitted that he did pee in the basket and did throw dirty paper in the basket.

The little boy could tell everyone was upset with him, but it was clear that he did not know why. Tears welled up in his eyes and he twisted his hands together. He began to sob. Finally he asked, "What did I do?"

Bob called his mother and she was horrified. She said that they had just bought an old farmhouse and the plumbing didn't work well. If much paper were thrown into the toilet it would overflow. She had warned her son to be careful about throwing paper in the toilet. As he hung up the phone, Bob understood why he threw the paper in the basket but didn't understand why he had to pee into the basket. He decided not to ask.

In May, the janitor would usually be at the principal's door with another problem: boys stuffing urinals with paper towels and then flooding the bathrooms. Bob knew from experience -- and the careful notes he kept -- that the culprits in this case would be the kids who were failing, who were not succeeding in school. They were acting from frustration and anger. Others kids were afraid of them and would never squeal on them. Outsmarting kids who thought they were clever was a challenge for the principal.

One method he used was to set up a meeting with each fifth grade class. The teachers set up the meetings and had the girls in the back of the room. The boys were in their seats. Bob walked in and looked at them sternly. They knew their principal was angry. At the sound of his stern words, the room became suddenly quiet. No more shuffling feet or tapping pens. They were listening.

Bob told them that every day this week the urinals in the boys' bathroom had been stuffed and the floor flooded. He glared at the boys. Then he watched their body language carefully.

Jimmy, an honor student, gave Jake a quick glance, but when Jake looked back at him he lowered his eyes.

Donny started to smirk, but quickly assumed a straight face.

Ivan, not afraid to show off a bit in front of his peers, asked with a face full of innocence, "Which bathroom was it?"

With anger in his voice, Bob told them that he wasn't answering questions. He added that if it happened again, the culprits would be caught and they would pay dearly. Turning abruptly, he left the room. In the hall, he jotted three names on a pad—Donny, Jake and Ivan. By acting the part of a stern authority figure, the principal was daring the boys to do it again. He knew they had to show their peers that they weren't intimidated by his threats and would do it again. That's why Donny gave his friends a quick smirk and why Ivan asked a question that everyone knew the answer to.

Bob gave the same speech in each fifth grade classroom and each time, added a few more names to his list. Then he waited for the inevitable.

That afternoon, a fifth grade teacher called on the intercom and told Bob that his speech didn't work; the bathroom was flooded again. Immediately, Bob switched on the intercom. He announced the nine names on the pad and told them to come to the office immediately. Soon the outer office was crowded with the boys—most of who sauntered in with a casual air.

"Jake, into my office." It was important to call the toughest kid into the office first. Most of the other kids, intimidated by Jake, wouldn't admit to anything until he did. Jake had large shoulders and dark eyes. He was scowling at Bob as he entered the office.

Bob told him that he knew for certain that he stuffed a urinal. Jake knew that all the boys in the outer office had stuffed the urinals. He knew he was caught and blurted out, "I only did it once."

"As you know you are in big trouble," said Bob, "I need to know the names of the others who did it." Normally Jake would never tell on one of his friends but now that he was caught, he didn't want to take all the blame. He rattled off a bunch of names.

One by one, Bob talked to the boys and each admitted their guilt. The tough part was still ahead. Bob had made such a big issue out of the urinal stuffing that he had to hand out a stiff punishment. He gazed sternly at the boys and suggested that they tell him what their punishment should be. Their answers came quickly:

"We should have to stay inside at lunch for the rest of the year."

"Call our parents and have them ground us for the rest of the year."

"Give us lots of homework every night for the rest of the year." (A smile crossed the principal's face at that one: these kids hadn't done homework all year).

"Make us stay after school every night for the rest of the year."

Bob was not surprised at the harshness of the punishment they suggested; children are always tough on themselves. All ended with "for the rest of the year" which was an eternity to them. Instead, Bob assigned them a week of sitting at a quiet table at lunch. They wouldn't be allowed to talk or go outside for the lunch period. If anyone talked, all would stay for another week. They felt it was unfair that all would be punished if one talked but they agreed to the punishment since they had expected it to be harsher.

They never knew how the principal knew they stuffed the urinals. They were left to wonder. That ended the bathroom problem for the year. Jake and his gang now guarded the lav against any kind of problems, afraid they would be blamed, and always looking around to find how the principal caught them. The teachers wished that the punishment had been longer; the playground had been peaceful for the week.

Certainly problems in schools have intensified far past stuffing urinals, throwing spitballs, or writing graffiti. More than ever principals, teachers, counselors, and parents need to work together to analyze patterns and figure out why kids do the things they do. Back in the 1970s keeping notes and observing patterns made a principal's job a lot easier. Today we think watching these patterns may be essential for keeping our children safe. The stakes are that much higher.

## Chapter 5
## Goblin Parade

Halloween was a magical day for children. They didn't have to fear monsters and ghosts; they joined them. Halloween was a holiday that gave each child a chance to take on a new character, a new personality. They tried to scare their friends. The impish grins and the giggling reminded teachers that Halloween was their holiday. It was a day when even the shyest young child could hide his insecurity behind a mask.

Orange and black colors decorated each classroom. Windows were covered with black cats, grinning jack-o-lanterns, and ghostly witches--each carefully cut from construction paper. Carved and painted pumpkins decorated the windowsills. Many classrooms had shocks of corn sitting on ~~bails~~ *BALES* of hay surrounded by a host of pumpkins. It looked like they had raided a farmer's field. By Halloween Day every bulletin board was covered with drawings of haunted houses and scary monsters.

Many teachers claimed to dread Halloween. It was a day when even well behaved children misbehaved. Yet, teachers dressed up and got excited on that special day. By lunchtime, they would complain that they were exhausted. Bob can remember coming into the faculty room and seeing teachers slumped back in their chairs, too tired to even talk. The door opened, a witch walked in and stood silently in the room for several moments and sighed, "It's so . . .so quiet in here." Everyone laughed!

Gloria said, "Wait until you see my costume!" She dug through her bag, pulling out pink leotards.

Another teacher kept complaining about how tired she was and how crazy the kids were acting. Then suddenly, she jumped out of her chair, leaving half of her sandwich, saying, "I have to hurry. My costume will take forever to put on."

She pulled out a red yarn wig: "Guess who I am?" In minutes, the worn-out teacher who didn't think she could make it through the afternoon was transformed into a colorful Raggedy Ann racing down the hall to pick her class up early.

Fourth grade teacher Norma was the exception. She tried to subdue the noise in her room with strict rules. Her booming and shrill voice could be heard echoing down the hall as she tried to restrain the children's holiday spirit. But most teachers, for all their complaints, were very creative. Halloween was a great day for creative writing or for artwork.

The teachers knew how important this day was for children. Some would read ghost stories and teach the history of Halloween. Many had the children write scary stories. Sam, a fifth grade teacher, invited Bob to listen to some of these stories. When he entered the room, shades were closed, the lights were off, and a child was reading

*Goblin Parade*

his story by flashlight. Danny's voice was clear and strong. He was one of the poorest reader in Sam's class. His lips moved slowly and with long pauses he sounded out each word. The rest of the class listened closely to the gory details of his story.

The Monster Pumpkin, donated by a local farmer, arrived a few days before Halloween. The huge pumpkin, weighing over 200 pounds, was taller than most kindergarten children. Each year the third grade held a contest. The child who painted the best pumpkin face on paper was given the privilege of painting the face on the Monster Pumpkin. Bob remembers the year that Claire, a little girl with ponytails, won the contest. The pumpkin was placed on a small flatbed cart and taken to the lobby. Barbara, the art teacher, and Claire were waiting. Like two engineers, Claire and Barbara directed the custodian where to place the pumpkin. Claire just stared at the monster and with a smile on her face, exclaimed, "And I'm going to paint it."

She was so excited. Like an accomplished artist, using long, bold strokes with her brush, she changed the pumpkin into a scary monster. Barbara heard many compliments as they painted and each time she wrapped her arms around Claire, gave her a big hug, and said, "Claire did all the work."

A kindergarten teacher brought her class to see it and told Claire that it was the scariest pumpkin she had ever seen. Claire's face beamed with pride. The children just stared at it as if it was alive, never saying a word.

The morning of Halloween, the Giant Pumpkin greeted the children as they enter school. They milled about talking and laughing as they passed this beautiful, but scary monster.

Almost every child who passed on their way from the bus to their classroom clutched a brown paper grocery bag. Some kids were very secretive about their costumes, wrapping their arms tightly around the crumpled bag. But many children would permit friends to peek in the bag, laughing and smiling at each other as they did so. The kindergarten kids wore their costumes from home to school. You could feel their excitement. It was wonderful to see how gently the older children treated the little ghosts and goblins. An older boy carefully lifted a little witch off the school bus. One hand was on her cape so it wouldn't get caught in the door. Even Donny left his normal gang to button up the back of his little brother Brad's devil costume.

Teacher's plans were flexible for this day including mostly games and scary stories. There was no quelling the noise. By lunchtime the noise level continued to rise throughout the school until it was a constant dull drone echoing through the hallways. It was amazing how quickly teachers recovered from their exhausting morning. The infectious spirit of Halloween spread through the rooms. Children transformed themselves into superheroes, witches, Little Red Riding Hood, Raggedy Ann and Andy or fairy tale princesses. They could be whatever they wanted to be. Surprisingly, often the cutest girls, instead of dressing up as a princess, wore the scariest costumes and the boys who often found their way into Bob's office wore the most elaborate outfits. Donny, one of these boys, dressed secretively in the bathroom. He reappeared as a jukebox with lights that changed colors and played music. Another child dressed as a crossword puzzle. Many were dressed as goblins, since all they needed was an old sheet and a little imagination. Store-bought costumes were common with monsters and skeleton often the theme.

We kept a box of costumes, donated by families, in the office for children in need. One time a grandmother stopped in the office about a week before Halloween and asked if we might have a need for some extra outfits for the poorer children. She pulled a little Red Riding Hood costume from the bag. It was adorable, all hand made, and probably from the turn of the century. It was beautiful and we wondered if we should accept it. She told Bob that it was hers when she was little. She continued to go through the bag. She had an Indian outfit with jagged cloth decorating each seam and a headband with genuine feathers. A little Bo Peep outfit including a curved wooden staff. She carefully folded each outfit and returned them to the flour sack. She looked concerned and a little sad: "Would these be nice enough for some child to wear?"

Then she took away all our doubt about accepting these treasures: "I'd be thrilled to think they were being worn again."

These gifts, with the others donated by parents, made Halloween special for many needy children. They were able to wear the costumes all day and to take them home for the evening festivities. They were always returned cleaned and in perfect repair.

It was easy to tell the children who had forgotten their costumes from the ones who didn't have one. The children who actually forgot wanted to call home. They would sit anxiously by the phone telling you where they had left their costumes and how they could call their mother or father to have them drop it off. The children who didn't have a costume looked sad and rejected as they stood in the doorway to the office.

Karen, for example, was the first child to be sent down to the office who truly needed something to wear. She stood stiffly by Alice's desk. "I forgot my costume," she said.

"Don't worry," said Alice, "We've got a whole box of extra costumes."

She and Karen began to sift through the costumes. Karen spotted the Little Red Riding Hood costume; her eyes lit up and hesitantly she asked if she could have that outfit. Alice helped her put it on.

## Goblin Parade

"You look great!" she told her. Karen, with tears in her eyes, wrapped her arms around Alice and gave her a big hug. After she left, Alice told Bob the story and added, "It just isn't fair. That little girl was just hurting inside."

Another Halloween tradition was the first grade visit to the nearby nursing home. Bev, a first grade teacher, had begun the tradition by asking Bob if she could take her class to visit the nursing home. Bob didn't know what to say at first. How would the children react to seeing patients in wheel chairs, their heads dropping to the side, their mouths open? He could imagine some patients wanting to reach out and touch the children.

Bev spoke up: "Bob, I know what you're thinking, but it would be a great experience for the little kids. Growing old is part of life. It is a shame we need to hide our old away where no one can see them."

Concerned, but knowing Bev, he agreed and knew she would work it out. Bob said he would send a note to parents telling them about the trip, and he agreed to babysit the children that couldn't go.

"Trust me, Bob. All the parents will let their kids go." Bev said. She was right.

On Halloween morning, Bob came down to Bev's classroom. The children were running around talking and laughing and acting the part of devils, witches, ghosts, Robin Hoods, and wolves. They didn't even notice their principal. Bev was in a long black dress with a flowing cape and a crooked witch's hat. She had painted her face green. She rested her broom on the wall next to the doorway while she worked at fastening the toy gun holster on one of her two cowboys.

Bob listened while she prepared the little ones for their visit to the nursing home. "If you feel scared or uncomfortable," she told them, "you can hang onto my dress."

We were soon on our way down the hallway. It took about ten minutes to walk to the nursing home. The supervisors met us at the entrance. We followed them through the newly polished hallways. The walls of the halls were covered with pictures of pumpkins, witches, and black cats. In almost every corner of the home was a bail of hay with shocks of corn. The nursing home had the same festive air of our school. It was obvious that the very young and very old are those who truly appreciated Halloween.

The first hallway we marched down was mostly empty. Some patients were in their doorways as we walked down the hall, but most of the doors were closed. Some of the children looked nervous as they stared at the residents. Bev stopped at one door. An old man sat in a wheel chair. He was a neighbor of Bev's when she was a little girl. His voice was low and raspy. He reached a frail and bony hand out to rest it on Bev's shoulder and shaking his head thanked her for bringing the children to his new home. She introduced her old friend to the class. Next they met Mary walking down the hall in her walker. Bev chatted with her for a few minutes before we moved on.

There were a few more stops to visit Bev's friends before we began the tour around the rest of the home. It was obvious Bev and the nursing home supervisors had prepared it so the children would meet Bev's friends before seeing the other patients. As we turned down the next hallway we began to see the sights that had turned me against this idea when Bev first suggested it. It was lined with patients, some in wheel chairs, and some on benches outside the rooms. A few of the children recoiled when they saw patients with their heads drooped to the side and their mouth wide open. Others meekly said, "Hello."

When some of the elderly patients reached out frail hands to touch the kids, some turned away. They grabbed hold of Bev's dress. Other children would carefully touch them. After a few minutes the children become comfortable with their surroundings. They paraded about timidly, yet seemed happy and proud. Brad, Donny's little brother, not fazed by anything, was poking at curtains and furniture with his plastic devil's pitchfork. Most of the patients were delighted to see the kids. Often tears appeared in their eyes and it was obvious that they would have liked to hug every one of those precious children.

We turned down the last hallway and marched out the front doors. Once outside the kids squealed and giggled, clutching each other's hands as they ran through the dried leaves that covered the green grass. It was time for the kids to go back to the school for the Halloween show, parade, and party.

Parents and grandparents had gathered in the cafeteria for the Halloween show. Each first and second grade class would sing a song, and then file out of the cafeteria for the next class to enter. "We Are Jack O Lanterns" was one of the favorites. It was a story about a little scary pumpkin that had teeth but didn't bite. They sang "Five Little Pumpkins sitting on a fence." Five students dressed as pumpkins sat on a table in front while the class began to sing:

*Five little pumpkins sitting on a fence.*
*The first one said, "Oh my, it's getting late."*
All the children pointed to their wrists.
*The second one said, "There are witches in the air."*
All put their hand above their eyes as if looking out over the cafeteria.
*The third one said, "But we don't care"'*
They shrugged and held their hands stretched out with their palms up.
*The fourth one said, "Let's run and run and run."*
The five pumpkins leaped off the table and began running around the stage. Their bellies bumped into each other and knocked each other down.
*The fifth one said, "I'm ready for some fun."*

## Goblin Parade

They all threw their hand excitedly in front of them. Then they formed an O with their finger and thumb and put it over their mouths.

*Oh went the wind and out went the lights.*

Lights were dimmed and the five little pumpkins began to crawl off the stage falling all over each other.

*And the five little pumpkins rolled out of sight.*

As the pumpkins crawled off the stage, the other student rolled their arms until they disappeared.

Another class sang a fall song, "Softly from the Tree Tops." These children had cut colored paper in the shape of leaves. As they sang, they dropped the leaves to make a lovely carpet of red, green and brown. As each color was sung, the children with that color dropped their leaves and watch them float to the floor.

The parents and grandparents smiled and laughed through the performance. No performance went without its unexpected moments. During one performance, a tiny girl rolled up her skirt until it showed her underpants. And during the last, Jake, a large boy, stood with his hand in his pockets and his mouth closed tightly. Two other boys were singing proudly but they were standing on the outside of their feet during the entire song. Others just smiled; looking at their parents, and never sang a word. Some just looked around mouthing words. Parents didn't care. They loved it.

The noise level in the building was peaking when the bell rang to signal the beginning of the parade. The doors opened and the traffic circle in front of school was quickly filled with excited children. The great mass of costumes moved forward in a singular motion, like a giant snake slithering from the lobby and into the driveway. Many parents and relatives were there to clap and cheer as the little fairies and witches walked by. The great Halloween parade involved marching three times around the circle in front of the school. It was exciting to see shy little kids transform themselves into a scary monster or a beautiful princess. Safe behind a mask, even the most withdrawn child would soon be racing and shouting.

One Halloween an unexpected downpour soaked all the children during the parade. Some of the cheap store-bought costumes fell apart. After the parade an angry parent called a teacher and said, "My Lucy can't go out trick-or-treating tonight because her costume got ruined today. If you can't control your class so that costumes aren't destroyed, then you shouldn't be teaching."

Feeling bad for the child, the teacher stopped at the local drugstore and found the exact same costume. Just before the witching hour, she went to Lucy's house, new costume in hand. Lucy answered the door. She was dressed as a most attractive tramp. She had on shabby pants, a huge pair of unmatched shoes, an old black hat, and a worn-out jacket. Her face was covered with make-

*Goblin Parade*

up, and all her teacher could see were her eyes, filled with excitement. She left with the new store costume still in its wrapper.

Following the parade the children returned to their classrooms and the hallways really filled with noise as the afternoon Halloween parties began. The judges gave the names of the winners to the teachers as they entered the building and the teachers awarded the winners in each category a certificate for ice cream from the cafeteria.

The day ended with all the children cleaning up after the parties and putting their costumes in their bags to take home. When the last bus finally pulled away from the parking lot, a peaceful silence fell over the building. Teachers were tired and glad the day was over but happy that it had been another fun-filled Halloween for their children.

"I'm going home and going straight to bed."
"I'm getting ready for round two."
"Can tomorrow be a teachers' holiday?"

The children enjoyed their day in school but were excited for the evening hours when they could parade around the village in their costumes, trick or treating. Minoa, like most small towns, would be filled with groups of children carrying pillowcases, bags and plastic pumpkin heads as the sun dropped and the pink sky darkened. The leaves had turned color and would tumble across the sidewalks and streets, pushed by the cool October breeze. At the fire barn, in the center of town, the firemen would serve cider and donuts to the parents and children and show cartoons in the basement.

After Halloween the monster pumpkin was given to a friend of Bob's. Our custodian brought it over to their house in his truck. About a week later, Bob's friend called and told him that that they were so excited about having the Monster Pumpkin they put it in the front living room window. Then she said, "Remember how cold it was last week? We set our thermostat higher those cold nights. The heat made the pumpkin explode. It went all over the living room rug and couch. I just finished cleaning it up and wanted to tell you thanks but no thanks."

Bob was horrified. Then she giggled, "The pumpkin looked like it had been in a fight. Seeds and pulp were all over the walls and floor. I just wanted to tease you. Having that pumpkin over the weekend was a thrill for my children. It was worth the mess it made."

Years have passed, but the tradition of visiting the principal's house continues. Bob still hands candy to trick-or-treaters in the village of Minoa, saying hello to more than a hundred children, including of course, Janine's four children.

## Chapter 6
## She's a Honey

The contribution of teaching is subtle yet significant. Often teachers never realize their accomplishments. They are too busy wiping away tears, settling arguments, and washing scraped knees. As a principal, Bob worked with many wonderful teachers who loved the children they taught and who believed that teaching was a vocation, a way to help their community. Many teachers look outside the classroom to see what the children are learning. Dorothy Rice Ford was one of these teachers.

She was an elementary school teacher for 42 years. Dorothy could have retired at the end of her $41^{st}$ year, making more money as a retiree than if she taught. Although he did not want to lose her as a teacher, Bob felt ethically obligated to tell her this. He called her into his office one day, and went over the details of her retirement plan with her. He noticed her blinking back tears.

When he was finished, she stood up, her lips quivering and in a loud voice said, "Bob Kinsella! You don't think I teach for money!" She continued to stare at him, and then in a voice barely audible asked, "Bob, can I have one more year with the little ones?"

Without saying a word, Bob walked around his desk and gave her a hug. "How lucky those little ones will be having you as their kindergarten teacher next year."

Her usual smile returned to her face, "Then I'll see you next year, Bob."

Dorothy had received tenure 39 years before. For 42 years she started each year as if it was her first. Every year was new and refreshing. She truly had 42 years of experience. Sadly we did have teachers that taught for years but only had one year of experience—they used the same plans, the same displays every year.

Dorothy knew that some of the children in her kindergarten class came from houses with plenty of books while other children had few. She asked parents to donate children's book--any type--for a project. Parents complied, sending in boxes and bags of books. Then Dorothy helped the children build bookshelves -- cardboard boxes decorated with paper. Dorothy displayed the books around the room and every day for a week each child could claim two books for themselves. At the end of the week they had a ten-book library at home in their special bookcase. During the year they could exchange books from home for book they liked at school.

Dorothy added, "What I like best is that the children after they read a book become salespersons for the book. They sit in the reading corner and tell others about their book. Pretty soon everyone wants to read that book."

One parent told her, "I just rediscovered that reading is fun and exciting again. I hadn't read a book in years until Johnnie set up his little 10-book library. We now read to Johnnie every night before he goes to sleep." Smiling she added, "We never realized the power of a book before—he is usually asleep before we finish the second book."

Other parents said they had always read a book before bedtime but now their child helped tell the story themselves as they looked at the pictures. Some said that some books were read so many times that the children would correct them if they missed a line.

Many kindergarten children weren't able to read. To encourage them, Dorothy had a daily story time. Children could bring in a book they liked and by pointing at pictures they told the story to the class. Some brought in a book they had memorized and read it, while other amazed their classmates by actually reading a book. Dorothy believed this was the way to get children to love book, handle books, and understand the story. She said, "When they learned to read, they relied less on pictures and more on words."

Nightly Dorothy's children went home with ideas that parents and children could expand on -- not simply fill in the blank sheets or coloring paper.

"Good teachers don't need busy work," Dorothy once said to Bob. "They need time. Time to expand the minds of growing children. Time to listen to the children, laugh with them, talk with them."

Dorothy always found time to do all these things. She believed that children wanted to learn. They just needed a helping hand to show them how exciting learning can be. There's nothing like self-motivation to help children excel. One summer she went to the nearby zoo and took pictures of the animals and made a bulletin board. The caption was, "Do you know who I am?"

She gave each child a list of the animals to take home. Parents were asked to take their child to the zoo to see how many animals on the list they could find. Her strategy worked, and most parents found the time to take their kids to the zoo. Dorothy promised to give the children a star for every animal they could find that she didn't. She said, "That cost me a lot of stars."

Even dedicated teachers like Dorothy had problems. One time, a mother called Bob and said that she was worried because her son had said that Mrs. Ford had slapped him. "I find it hard to believe because Mrs. Ford seemed like such a kind teacher," the parent said, "And I am worried because he is wearing braces so a slap could really hurt him or the braces."

Bob knew it wasn't true. Mrs. Ford would never hurt one of her children.

When Bob went down to talk to Dorothy, she was relaxing in her chair staring out the windows of her room at the small playground framed by the U shape of two wings of the school. It was a perfect setting for a kindergarten room, and Dorothy loved it. She was surprised but not upset when Bob told her about the call.

"Bob, you know better. And I know Greg. He just wouldn't make up a story like that." She had a puzzled look on her face. She brushed a strand of hair from her face with her knuckle. "Call the Mom and let's straighten this out now."

Bob knew she was right. Many problems can be resolved if parent and teacher sit down and talk. He made the phone call and soon Greg and his mother joined Dorothy and Bob in the principal's office.

Greg's mom said, "When Greg came into the house from school, he said Mrs. Ford had slapped him in the face."

Dorothy was visibly shaken. She had expected the matter would be resolved before Greg's mother reached the school.

Greg jumped out of his chair and said, "Mommy. I didn't say that she slapped me in the face!" He looked straight into his mothers' eyes. His little hands were shoved nervously in his pant pockets. "She wouldn't do that! She loves me." His voice was shaky and full of worry.

"Why did you tell me that she slapped you?"

"She did! She patted me on the back to hurry me off the playground. Mommy, you know what a poke I am."

## Both Sides of the Desk

Dorothy smiled. "But the cutest little poke in kindergarten," she laughed. She turned to Greg's mother. "Why don't you come down to the classroom and see the art projects we've been working on?" The three of them left my office, the two women chatting while Greg ran ahead to show his mother where the art project was.

Dorothy often invited Bob to visit her classroom and share time with her children. She was always relaxed during his visits and he always left with new ideas to share with others. One observation was different. She told Bob, "In the teachers' room yesterday I heard some teachers talking about how they hate it when children tattle." She hesitated for a moment then added, "I strongly believe that we shouldn't be upset with these children but should encourage them. I am appalled with the mafia code of silence thrust upon children."

Her face paled with anger. "Before I leave this school, I want you to clearly understand my position. Teachers have an obligation to break this code of silence among children."

She asked Bob to observe her lesson on tattling. He sensed her anger about the topic, but didn't really understand it. But he trusted that it was something worth listening to. He said: "Let me know when and I'll be there."

A few days later, Bob watched from the back of the classroom as Dorothy stood in front of the children with her hands clenched tightly together, in an unconscious betrayal of her nervousness. It was the first time he had seen her tense while teaching children. He just couldn't understand why she would teach a lesson on tattling and certainly couldn't understand why it was so important to her.

Dorothy started the lesson with a story about herself when she was a new teacher. "I was teaching a fifth grade class. A large boy in the class had been sticking the other kids with a needle. The children were afraid of him so no one tattled on him. My principal came into the classroom and asked me to come out into the hall. A girl that the boy stuck with a needle got blood poisoning and was in the hospital. Her parents were furious that I hadn't stopped the boy from hurting other children. The principal was so mad that he was thinking of firing me." At this point she interjected. "That principal was not Mr. Kinsella. Imagine if I had been fired I never would have been a teacher and I would have missed all the fun teaching children like you, for over forty years. I promised that day, that no child in my class would ever be afraid to tell me anything in class."

She asked if any of them had told their mother about something an older brother or sister had done. Many nodded, "Yes." Then she asked what their older brother or sister called them after their mother was out of sight. Many said they yelled at them, threatened to hit them, wouldn't play with them. One boy stood up. He turned his palm up on his left hand and extended his index finger, then he rubbed his right index finger over the top of the left index finger and at the same time said over and over again in a rhythmic way, "tattle tale, tattle tale, tattle tale."

She looked into his eyes and said, "You really felt bad when they said that to you."

The boy nodded in agreement.

"Boys and girls, I never want you to call anyone a tattle tale. I think it's mean, even though sometimes it does make you mad. But remember the boy who was sticking children with a pin. Would you call one of your classmates, who told his teacher about this, a tattle tale?"

All the children understood the importance of telling in this case.

Then she asked them to think of things they should tell their teacher. Naturally, stabbing a child with a pin was the first answer. But they came up with other things as well:

      Fighting.
      Hitting
      Jabbing with a pencil
      Talking
      Throwing papers on the floor
      Copying

She wrote the answers on the board as they said them. Then she read them off the board one at a time and asked if they would tell the teacher if this happened. Surprisingly they seemed to understand that incidents that could injure another child should be reported and maybe talking, throwing paper on the floor and copying didn't need to be told to the teacher. They understood that if they were concerned, they should come to her desk and tell her. They should never yell it out so the whole class could hear. Then she said in almost a whisper, "Remember, no matter what you tell me, I'll never get mad at you. In fact I'll thank you for telling me."

That lesson, learned while standing in the back of Dorothy's classroom, changed forever my idea of what a tattletale was. In fact, Janine uses a version of this lesson with her college students, explaining to them her worry about what will happen if a student drinks enough to put himself in danger and other students are so worried about covering up the incident to protect the student that no one will get help to get the drunken student to the emergency room. Even at the college level, the stigma of being a tattletale is still powerful and dangerous.

Dorothy did retire at the end of her $42^{nd}$ year and then worked daily with Alex, her husband, operating Rice's Grocery Store. Years later, long after the store had closed, Bob was getting a haircut at Louie's barber's shop. While Louie was cutting his hair, they started talking about Louie's school days, and Bob asked, "Was Mrs. Ford one of your teachers?"

"Yes, I had Mrs. Ford," he said excitedly, "and she never forgot me." He paused the hair cut to tell Bob the story.

He was returning from a day of deer hunting with his younger brother, and they decided to stop at Rice's Store. He was at the counter paying, when the woman cutting meat yelled out, "Mr. Cretaro, aren't you going to speak to your old teacher?"

Louie looked up. It was Mrs. Ford in jeans, cutting meat. Surprised, he asked, "Mrs. Ford, you remember me?"

"Louie Cretaro, you were one of my favorite kindergarten students."

Louie then added, "Maybe she said that to all her students, but I was thrilled!"

Teachers know good teaching and so do children. Bob overheard a first grader talking with a second grader about his teacher. Emphatically he said, "She's mean." The second grader had the same teacher the year before and he smiled. It was a knowing smile. He then shared with the first grader the wisdom of an older student. "She seems mean at first, but she really is a honey."

Mary, a second grade teacher, was the first teacher that Bob hired at Minoa. Like Dorothy, Bob often visited her classroom, not for evaluation but for knowledge that he could share with other teachers. Her one reading goal was to get children to develop a love for reading. In one observation

*She's a Honey*

Bob noted that instead of having children read out loud, a common practice referred to as "Round Robin Reading" she had them read a paragraph or a page silently, and then close their book on their finger while she asked questions like: "What do you think will happen next? What does the author want you to know? Do you like the way author tells the story? Would you like to read another story by this author?"

When they finished the story, she asked: "Why or why didn't you like the story? How would you have ended the story?"

She told Bob, "Children must be involved in the story not just the words. They must be moved by the word and be able to share these feeling with their classmates. Developing a love of reading is an elementary school's most important goal."

Mary had a keen sense of humor and had the rare gift of being able to laugh at herself. When children finished their work they were able to go the learning center in the back of the room. It was a challenging center that offered creative problems for children. The math center had a problem that completely stumped one of her best students. The problem was: A farmer, his dog, and six cows were going down the road. How many feet were on the ground?"

The girl tried many times but never did get the right answer. School ended and Mary could see that the child was still puzzled about the problem.

The next day she rushed into the room and exclaimed, "I got the right answer now?"

The smile on her the girl's face clearly told Mary that this time she had the right answer and asked, "What is the answer?"

"Zero!"

Mary, puzzled said, "I'm sorry but that wrong."

The little girl pulled out a picture she drawn. It showed a farmer, his dog, and six cows in a wagon.

Sam Falise, a fourth grade teacher, also loved teaching and spent hours planning his day. Timetables were taught in third grade but most of his students didn't know them when they started fourth grade. In fact he discovered that many left elementary school not knowing them. He knew that math, unlike reading, was a linear subject. It was built in steps. Each step prepared students for the next level and in sequential step they progressed through the math curriculum.

Many of his children intuitively understood complex problems and he would challenge them with thought problems instead of pages of math problems they already knew. Sam knew that having children do a page of math problems that they already knew bored them and even turned some of them off on math. He often found students who understood the more complex problems but constantly got them wrong because of a simple times table error. He was afraid that many of these students who would be good math students would become frustrated and consider themselves failures. He was determined that his student wouldn't fail for not knowing the tables.

Every week they studied part of the table. Every Friday was test day and if every child got 100 they would have a popcorn party. The children loved the challenge. They even tested each other during free time and even at recess so that all passed—they never missed a Friday without a popcorn party. Bob once asked, "Sam, do all the children really get a hundred every week?" He just smiled but by January all his kids did know their tables.

Sam pushed for student to excel but he was always concerned with children who were struggling. He would study these children and their work, talk to them and try to find out why they weren't learning. He said, "Don't just look at test scores, look at the child."

One of Sam's students, a boy named Chucky, was a quiet boy who wore the same clothes almost every day. The clothes smelled. And it was clear that his hair had not been washed in weeks. When Chucky began failing, Sam was concerned. He knew that Chucky could do better. He told Bob, "He is so alone. The children shun him. If only his father would clean him up and buy him some decent clothes, he would be a good student."

He said, "I'm going to buy him some new clothes if he wants them."

Then he added, "Would you talk to him and see if he would wear them?"

Bob hesitated, thinking that this whole thing could backfire, but Sam was so determined to help Chucky that he didn't want to say no.

Sam sent Chucky to the office with a note. Bob asked the boy to sit down.

"Mr. Falise says you are having some problems in class. He said you're a bright child, and he wants to see you do well. He thinks you are capable of doing your work."

Chucky was sullen and angry. "Yeah, I know how to do it." His voice was low. He turned his head and began to cry. His sobs were loud and frequent. Bob sat down next to him and put his arm around him. Even though his reaction was instinctive, he had to fight the impulse to move away instantly as the smell of his unwashed body and filthy clothes struck him.

Chucky's crying subsided into light gasps. "All the kids hate me. I'm not like the other kids." The tears left streaks on his dirty face. "My clothes are dirty and everyone calls me stinky. Our washing machine ain't working, and Dad will only let us have a bath once a week. He's trying to save money. Besides my clothes are so old it wouldn't make any difference."

"How would you feel if you had new clothes?"

His big brown eyes widened, "New clothes?" There was suppressed excitement in his voice--and a little awe. "I've never had new clothes."

"After lunch, go to the nurse's office. Mrs. Luddington will measure you and tomorrow she will have new clothes for you."

Sam didn't want Chucky to know that he bought the clothes. The nurse said, "Sam's such a great guy. Maybe I'll even like that darned mustache after this."

Chucky's eyes shone as he left my office. He stopped at the door, "Do I have to take the clothes home?" Bob knew what he was asking. He wanted to keep the clothes a secret from his father.

The next morning Chucky got up early, and walked two miles to school. He wanted to be there when the nurse came in.

Jane was thrilled. "Bob, you can't believe how excited he was to see those new clothes." Sam had bought three complete sets of clothes, including new underwear. "He even wanted to pick up the clothes at the end of the day to wash and iron them." She convinced him that it might be better if she did it. She wanted to be part of this adventure.

Jane gave Chucky a bottle of shampoo, a bar of soap, and a towel. Larry our custodian took Chucky to the boy's locker room to clean up and put on his new clothes. Larry, all excited, stopped in the office afterwards to give a thumbs up. His grin lit up his face. He looked like a little child who knew he had done something right.

Every day Chucky took a shower and changed into his new clothes. He looked like a different boy, handsome and clean in the new shirt and pants, but always, before going home, he'd stop in the nurse's office and change back into his old clothes. Sam was amazed in the change. "He does his work right away now and he seems to be making friends with some of the boys in his reading group. Even Carol in the cafeteria noticed the big change. "What dimples he has." It was the first time anyone of the staff had seen him smile.

For two months, Chucky was a different boy. Then the inevitable happened. His father found out and he was furious. He demanded that it be stopped. Linda, his sister, had squealed on him. Chucky didn't go to the nurse's office for his clothes the next day—nor any day after that. He returned to his old way. Homework was never done and his dimples disappeared forever.

## Chapter 7
## Death of a Teacher

    Sam Falise was a fourth grade teacher who had a natural way of teaching that was inviting to his students. He wanted his children not to just memorize answers to pass a test but to take with them information that would become part of their lives. He was determined that his class would learn about nature in the woods, not from a book. He was one of the teachers who worked hard to transform a forgotten area behind the children's playground into a nature trail.
    When the nature trail, a mulch trail leading through the woods, was ready to be used, Sam invited Bob to join his class for their first walk on it. When Bob arrived in the fourth grade classroom, the rows of children were squirming excitedly, and Sam sat on the edge of his desk, smiling below his moustache. He posed a question, "Now what will you do when we enter the woods?" One boy in the corner shot his hand into the air.
    "Look and listen," the boy said.
    "Good Dennis. This nature trail will be our outdoor science lab. In any science lab you must use all your senses to learn. You must listen to the sounds and pay close attention to the smells. And watch carefully to see insects and even animals."
    Sam told the class that in just a few minutes they would be making history. They would be the

first class to walk on the new nature trail. He went to the board and wrote the words "The Unmasking of the Poison Trail" in bold chalk letters. "As I told you, each visit we make to the nature trail will have a different assignment. The assignment for today is this riddle. I want you to think about these words while we travel through the woods. I want you to solve this riddle."

As the children walked down the hallway, they talked excitedly about what they would see. Some thought there would be people along the trail with masks to scare them. Others thought there might be bears or deer in the woods.

As we neared the woods we could see the newly spread wood chips that outlined the trail. The woodchips followed the path made by a pipe that carried off rainwater from the school grounds to a pond in the woods. The smell of the wood chips was pungent but pleasant.

We trudged along silently. At the pond the trail veered off to the right along its banks. The children were anxiously looking around. We passed red maples and ash trees with hairy vines, and passed many dead and fallen trees in various stages of decay. There was a surprisingly huge sugar maple tree standing on a knoll just to the left of the trail. Its mammoth branches reached toward the sky and leaned outward, sagging down slightly at the edges to form a huge crown. We followed the trail around the back of the pond, completing a full circle. The children waited silently for their teacher

to speak. Some watched the water flow under the log bridge.
"Does anyone understand the saying 'The Unmasking of the Poison Trail' now?" Sam asked.
Most of the children just shook their head. After a few moments Tommy, a blonde-haired boy with glasses, raised his hand.
"What do you think, Tommy?"
"Poison ivy. It's all over."
Sam smiled. "Excellent observation. Did anyone else see the poison ivy?" Many hands went up. "When we take our second trip through maybe you could point some poison ivy out to us, Tommy. And maybe you could teach us how to recognize it. Poison ivy makes you itch so avoid it."
Sam walked to where the trail jutted down the bank of the creek. "But that is only one part of the riddle. Does anyone know the rest?" All were silent.
"Okay, listen carefully to my clues," he said. "What you are going to learn is usually taught in the ninth grade. They learn it from a book and most forget it. But I hope our lesson today will become part of your life forever. And then when you are in the ninth grade you can think back to how you learned this through the riddle 'the unmasking of the poison trail.'"
"In social studies we have been studying manufacturing. What is manufacturing? Kathy?"
"Making something," she said. "Something that others can use."

"Good. Today we are going to learn about manufacturing in the woods." There were some giggles. "Seriously, class--manufacturing takes place all around us." He walked over to a small sapling at the edge of the trail. It was not more than five feet tall and had frail branches and pale green leaves. "All green plants, including trees, use a process called photosynthesis. It's a long word and not important that you remember it. But every spring the plant makes chlorophyll. Chlorophyll is what gives all plants and leaves their green color. Chlorophyll combines with sunshine and the air to make sugar and give off oxygen. And what do we use oxygen for?"

"To breathe," a boy yelled.

"Of course. So if we think of each green plant as a manufacturing plant, what do the plants make?"

"Oxygen," Linda said.

"And who uses the oxygen the plants produce, Mandy?" Sam looked to a girl in the back.

"We do!" she said.

"Excellent," Sam said. "So green plants make sugar and purify the air by giving off oxygen and each of us needs oxygen to breathe."

Next Sam talked about these tiny manufacturing plants and the importance of trees to our environment. The children were getting more excited as the discussion continued. The impact of the trail had taken hold.

"This still doesn't seem to answer the question about unmasking, though," he said. "Let's continue with photosynthesis. Green plants are sensitive to both light and temperature. As fall approaches, the sun moves south and shortens our sunlight causing the temperature to drop. The plants sense this and begin to shut down. They know winter is coming. Have you ever seen your mother run to the grocery store before a big snow storm?"

Many of the children nodded. Upstate New York was known for its severe snowstorms. "Well, plants do the same thing. When they have stored enough food for the winter, they shut down. As the trees shut down, they lose their chlorophyll. What did I say chlorophyll did?"

"It makes air?" a girl answered timidly.

"Yes. Chlorophyll combines with sunshine and air to make oxygen. But it also gives plants their green color. So when the plants shut down, the leaves lose their chlorophyll, removing the green mask from the leaves." He looked around to ensure the clue had been properly placed. "Once the green mask has been removed, other colors appear. Sort of like taking off a sweater with a shirt underneath. That is why in the fall the leaves turn their many colors. And that's what makes fall such a beautiful time of the year in this area." Sam waited several moments before continuing. "Let's think about it again. Tommy was right when he said the 'poison' was for poison ivy. Can anyone now tell me what the unmasking part is?"

Many hands were raised. Sam nodded to Sue, a girl with dark skin and big brown eyes. "Leaves wear a green mask during the spring and summer. But in the fall they remove their mask and show their many colors." Sam smiled, obviously surprised by her beautiful answer to his difficult question.

"That was wonderful, Sue," he said. The other children clapped. "All right, are you ready now to walk the trail again." The children nodded. "This time we will talk and share our ideas."

We began the walk along the bank of the creek again. Sam stopped at a dead tree that had fallen alongside the trail. We passed the tree in silence on our first trip. This time Sam knelt down and asked the kids if they thought the tree had any value now. Many just shook their heads no and some even laughed.

"Never forget, all trees have value. This dead tree is the ultimate in recycling. When it was alive it took resources from the earth so it could grow, make sugar and gives off oxygen for you and me to breathe. And now that it is dead, it is decomposing and giving back to the earth a rich soil so that other trees can grow. Look closely," he said. His pudgy hands brushed aside some dead chips of wood and then sunk into the moist and rotted flesh of the tree. Insects scurried for cover. "See those little worm-like creatures with their many legs." He pointed to one with a finger. It crawled slowly across the exposed wood. "Those are called centipedes."

"Notice the bugs that are shaped like a tiny pill box. What do you think they are called?"

"Pill box bugs?" someone said.

"Yes," Sam said. "Now watch what happens when I touch the bug." He did so and the bug curled into a tiny gray ball. "Anyone know why?"

"For protection?" Jerry answered.

"Exactly. Good observation."

Sam moved back some of the grass growing along the sides of the tree. He pointed to a white thread-like substance and told them it was fungi that were helping the tree decompose. He said another type of fungi that appears later in the decomposition process is the mushroom. The children were quick to spot mushrooms. One boy said excitedly, "I'll bet a tree died there."

Further down the trail Tommy pointed out the poison ivy growing on the red maple trees. Sam complimented him and then added, "Look carefully at the vine. It is very hairy looking. This is an identifying characteristic of poison ivy. Often people look at grape vines and think it is poison ivy. But grape vines are smooth, not hairy. Poison ivy vines are not dangerous to touch unless the liquid inside gets on your skin. I'm sure some of you have gotten the liquid on your skin." There were nods. "Well, for those of you who haven't, it causes a severe skin irritation. So, class, what should you do when you spot poison ivy." The children quickly told Sam they should avoid it. "Notice the three red leaves." He pointed to each as he spoke. "The ivy has lost its green mask." They all nodded in agreement.

Next we came to a newly cut tree. The children all seem to know they could tell the age of the tree by counting the rings. He asked if they could tell anything else. Some actually knew that the width of the rings denoted the type of growing conditions the tree had that year. Tommy pointed to a very narrow ring and said, "It must have been a dry summer that year."

They continued down the path and stopped in front of the huge sugar maple tree. It was the only sugar maple on the trail. They talked about the tree and decided it was the lone survivor from the farmer's tilled land. It survived because it grew on a little knoll away from the wet ground the red maples and ash tree thrived on. "Next spring we will tap the tree for maple sugar. In fact, I'll even promise you a pancake breakfast with our very own syrup." That was the climax of the field trip.

"Really? Can we?"

Back in their room, Sam said, "Class, this was an exciting day for me. Every child in school should do and see what you did today. Show your parents the trail. Invite them as your special guests, and share with them what you learned." He then pointed to the back of the room to the reading table and said, "I have arranged some books to help you learn more about trees and plants and insects." The little heads turned quickly to the back table. The books were stacked neatly in piles around the circular table. "I hope you get a chance to look at them and talk about them with your classmates. Remember, you are the pioneers for this trail. It's up to you to encourage others to use this wonderful resource."

It was late September that year when Sam told Bob he was having problems with his vision. The doctors determined it was a pituitary problem and he should have surgery as soon as possible. Sam put the surgery off until the Monday after Halloween; he didn't want to miss Halloween with his kids. He treated the subject casually, yet he was nervous. We knew that any surgery near the brain was serious, but he said the doctor thought he would be back in school in less than a week.

The morning of the surgery, he sent a message to the class praising them for being so good for Mrs. Roberts, his substitute. He wanted them to know that he was proud of them and they could have their regular popcorn party on Friday. Sam was still thinking of his kids first and was anxious to be back with them.

Like the kids, Bob assumed Sam would be back in the classroom in no time. When Alice rushed into his office Friday morning, he wasn't expecting the news she had just gotten over the phone from Sam's wife.

"It's bad news, Bob," she paused and then just said bluntly, "Sam died this morning."

"What do you mean? I just told his class he would be back on Monday."

"He's dead, Bob. I just got off the phone with his wife," she spoke quietly, but she was trying not to cry. "Bob, I'm sorry. I'm so sorry."

"Alice, I need to be alone for a few minutes."

"Is there anything I can do?"

"No, that's okay."

"Should I tell his class? The staff?"

"I'll handle it, Alice. I just need a few minutes."

She left and gently shut the door.

Bob tried to think of all the things that would need to be done. The substitute was only scheduled for a week. Who could step in for the rest of the year? The children would need to be told. And the staff would take it just as hard as the children.

Maybe it was a mistake. Bob thought, "Maybe I should call the hospital and confirm." But he knew he was only fooling himself.

He wished he knew what he was supposed to do. What was the right thing to do as his friend and principal? Bob was used to solving problems by relying on what he'd learned from past experience, but there was no experience to draw on now. He felt alone.

## Death of a Teacher

He wondered how Sam's wife was taking this. She helped out in the chorus, and everyone teased Sam about his voice. Gloria said he sounded a little like Elvis singing opera. And how could anyone forget his mustache? Bob often suspected that Sam didn't like the mustache himself but it had become such a conversation piece that he didn't dare shave it.

Bob thought about the note Sam had sent to the children in his class. And he knew what he needed to do -- think about the children. That is what Sam would have wanted. His own grief at losing a friend could come later. Sam's class came first. They were expecting their teacher back Monday.

When he was able to control his voice, he left the inner office to talk with Alice. He admired her resiliency. Bob knew she was feeling the loss as deeply as he yet while he had sought refuge behind a closed door, she had gone right back to work. She was at her desk typing away and handling the people that are always coming in and out of the office. She gave him an anxious, maternal look and reached over to squeeze his arm.

"I need to meet with the staff after school, I'll tell them then."

"I'll set up the meeting," Alice responded. Then she looked up. "Bob, what about John?"

John was very close to Sam and his wife. "I'll tell him first." It was almost dismissal time.

Bob walked down to John's room and motioned for him to come into the hall. He guessed his eyes were red but John didn't seem to notice.

"What's up?" he asked casually. Bob could tell he was still thinking about the lesson he'd interrupted. He had a broad smile on his face.

During the short walk down the hallway Bob had tried to think how Alice had told him and if there was anything she might have said to make it easier. There was no way to soften the fact that Mike was dead.

"John, we just got a call from Cindy Adams. Sam died this morning."

John's smiled faded. When Bob finished saying the words, he looked away, wishing he hadn't had to say them. The hall was very quiet and a few muffled whispers came from the classroom.

"When?"

"This morning."

John looked at the meter stick in his hands and turned it over gently several times.

"I can't believe it. I never expected." He fell silent.

None of those old clichés would console someone for the sudden loss of a friend. Bob remained silent.

After several moments the classroom began getting noisy. While Bob heard the voices and the laughter, his insides felt hollow and he had neither the energy nor the desire to do anything about it. The children seemed a world away. John stood in the empty hallway, gripping the ruler in his hand, his face steady and calm.

"Go sit in the faculty room for a bit," Bob said. "I'll take your class for this last twenty minutes."

"No. I'm okay," he said. "I can teach. It's almost dismissal time anyway." He turned abruptly to go back into the classroom but paused, "Thanks for coming down to tell me, Bob."

At the faculty meeting that night, teachers were talking and wondering why they were having a faculty meeting on a Friday. It's something that Bob never did. He could hear the anxiety in their voices. But no one was prepared for the news.

"We just got word from Cindy," Bob told them, "Sam died this morning."

Shocked and silent, the circle of faces stared back at Bob. Many were crumpling into tears. Bob fought to control his voice, "The children will be scared, they won't understand and will have questions for us and we need to have the right answers Monday morning."

Slowly, in a dazed sort of way, they discussed what little they knew about what had happened. One by one the teachers found their voices again:

"Some of the children will already know when they come in Monday,"

"Others won't know."

"The obituary will be in the newspaper Saturday."

"We'd better make sure that the kids who haven't heard, hear it from us and not from some kid in the lunch room."

"Each homeroom teachers should greet their children at the door Monday and be prepared to answer questions about Sam's death."

Mrs. Roberts, the substitute, was in tears. Both hands were over her face.

"We need to answer their questions and give them time to grieve."

"Yes, we need to have a talk with the children in Sam's class."

Jane, the school nurse, agreed to lead a class discussion. She was sensitive, perceptive and sympathetic. She would be the perfect person. The children trusted and respected her and the staff felt that the children might be more likely to open up if she spoke with them.

Bob had already contacted Pat, the school psychologist. She was at the meeting and agreed to help Jane.

After the meeting Jane, Pat, and Mrs. Roberts met in the principal's office. Alice joined us since she would be manning the office and the phone Monday. We tried to anticipate children's questions, and we talked of ways to help the children understand and cope with the tragedy. We agreed that it was important that after meeting with the children, we'd meet again to review what happened.

Monday morning, Bob stood outside Sam's classroom with Pat and Jane, talking to the children as they arrived.

Sam's obituary had been in the paper over the weekend; many of the children had heard the news from either their parents or from the other children on their bus, but many had questions or worries.

"Will he come back?"

"Will he be buried?" asked one boy, "My grandpa was buried."

"Will he be buried tomorrow?"

Some of the children had no questions but walked quietly into their classroom. There was not the usual banging of lunch boxes and desktops.

Once the bell had rung, Bob left Jane and Pat with Sam's class. It was nearly 10 am when they showed up in his office to report on the discussion they'd had with the kids. They both looked somber and tired when they arrived and took chairs in the office. Mrs. Roberts, they said, was with the class.

Bob took notes as they talked.

Jane started, "First we pushed all the desks back." Then with the children sitting all in a group on the floor, they began the discussion. Jane told them that Mr. Falise died Friday and she was sure they had questions about his death. She said the purpose of this class meeting was for them to talk and ask questions.

"The children wasted no time," Pat said. "I thought we would have to work to get them to open up." But the children started quickly asking questions.

How did Mr. Falise die?
When did he die?
Where will he be buried?
What happens at a funeral?

"Some of the children had had previous experiences with death," Jane said.

"My little brother died," Holly told the class. "I went to the grave and saw the stone. It was a big stone that said Baby Nelson on it."

And then a girl in the class asked what her brother's name was. "Baby Nelson," Holly repeated.

Pat told the class he must have been a new baby who died before a name was picked out for him.

"Tracy asked if little kids go to funerals. It was clear that she was worried about it."

"I told her it depends. Some children are upset by funerals and other children aren't, and children should talk to their parents about whether or not to go."

Jane asked them if any of them had ever been to a funeral. Tommy raised his hand. "I went to my grandmother's funeral. They put her in a black car and drove to the grave place and buried her in the ground with flowers on top."

Another little boy told about his cat dying. They buried her in the back yard.

"I told them that everyone has to die sometime but most don't die until they are old. To that Holly said: 'Mr. Falise wasn't old.'"

"Then Bobbie," Jane said, "who had been silent the whole discussion shouted out, 'He told us he was coming back.' And most of the kids nodded in agreement. That was the first time I'd seen that they were angry too."

Pat told them that Mr. Falise really thought he was coming back. He didn't know he was going to die. A girl asked, "Why didn't he go to the doctor and get better?"

"Mr. Falise was in the hospital," Jane said. "And many doctors looked at him. They did everything they could but he still died."

"I guess what was difficult for me," Jane said, "was trying to help the children understand the permanence of death. We talked about the pets they had that died--and they seemed to understand death was permanent for then. But they wanted to make an exception for humans. I was struck with the fact that these children were facing mortality for the first time--and thinking how strange it must be for them. Some of the children kept saying that they wished Mr. Falise could come back to life."

Pat tried to explain that usually we feel sad when we lose someone we love, and we wish they could come back and be with us. But that can't happen no matter how much we wish it. The class was silent for a few moments until Brenda raised her hand.

"I felt sad when I found out."

"'I felt sad too," Jane said.

Then she asked if anyone else felt sad. Most of the children nodded.

"What does being sad feel like?" Pat asked.

"It hurts in my stomach, It's a heavy feeling inside me." Roy said, hitting his fist to his chest to demonstrate.

One girl said that she had cried. Jane told her she cried too and added, "Some times I feel better when I cry."

"I could tell many of the kids were astonished." Jane said, "But I think it is important that they know it is all right to cry."

"'How long do you feel sad inside?' Terri asked.

Pat told her that it lasts a while, but as time goes by you start to feel better.

Teresa said, "When my dog Sam died, I felt terribly sad and cried and cried, but after a while I didn't feel so sad."

"Time really helps. And sometimes, when someone dies, it helps to do something for the family," said Pat.

Suddenly George burst our crying. Pat put her arm around him. He whispered in her ear that he hated Mr. Falise last week for keeping him after school. She told him we all feel that way at times about people we love. But he kept crying and said, "I didn't mean it. I didn't want to hurt Mr. Falise." He pushed his head into her blouse and wrapped his arms around her.

"George, we all get mad at people we love but that can't make them sick or, worse, die. Mr. Falise died because he had a sickness doctors couldn't cure. You had nothing to do with his sickness." Pat told him.

"Kelly suggested that we write to Mr. Falise's wife and tell her how we feel sad. I told her that was a good idea and suggested we might want to collect money as well to donate to a charity. Then a little dark-haired girl--I don't remember her name--asked if we had to pick something now. I told her, no, that they could think about it and talk with Mrs. Roberts tomorrow."

Jane and Pat said the discussion went on for another hour. They were surprised that the kids acted so sophisticated. They saw none of the rudeness or giggling that you usually have when little kids talk.

"Little Tammy cried most of the time. Peter didn't participate at all. He started playing with the aquarium near the window."

"We just let him play," Jane said. She knew Peter and his family. "His grandfather passed away recently."

"I guess I am still a little worried about George," Pat said. "He seemed to understand what

I told him but I have a feeling he still feels he is at least partly at fault. I'll talk to his parents this week."

Toward the end of the hour some of the boys joined Peter looking at the fish in the aquarium. Tracy said, "The boys like the fish more than they do Mr. Falise."

"Actually," Jane said. "I was surprised at how long the talk lasted. Kids that age have such short attention spans."

Pat asked just before they left, "Do you feel better?" One little boy said he felt better but was still very sad.

Sam was buried on a Tuesday afternoon. Many staff members went to the funeral. None of Sam's children attended. It would have been difficult for the staff to see those little faces staring over the pews of the church. Bob assumed that parents discussed it with their children and decided it was best that they didn't attend.

Thursday, Mrs. Roberts stopped Bob in the hall at lunchtime. "Could you come to our room sometime today?" she asked. "The kids want to talk to you about Mr. Falise."

Janie and Tracy were elected as the spokespersons. They stood in the front of the classroom, close together for support. Their arms touched lightly as they shuffled their feet nervously.

"Mr. Kinsella," Tracy began, "Monday when we all talked, Mrs. Ludington said we could do something for Mr. Falise's family and said we could think about it. Well, we thought about it and we decided that we will write a letter to Mrs. Falise and tell her how much we liked Mr. Falise."

"Tracy, Mrs. Falise will like that."

"We also decided," Janie said, "that we would like to do something that would always remind us of Mr. Falise." There were several nods from the other children as she spoke. "We would like to take a collection from our class and buy a tree. We can plant it right outside this room. Right near the windows. It will be like Mr. Falise is standing outside and looking in at us." She looked at her principal and asked, "Can we?"

Bob's eyes watered and he said, "And I'll help you plant it."

The tree would mean more to these children than any funeral.

Early that spring we held the commemoration. The ground had begun to thaw several weeks before and Larry, our custodian, had gone out early in the morning and dug the hole outside Sam's class. The children watched him digging, and Mrs. Roberts said there was a strange silence in the room as they watched his every move.

Late morning when the sun was high over the trees in the forest that bordered the school Bob joined Mrs. Roberts, Jane, Pat, Sam's class and Gloria, their music teacher, outside the fifth grade wing. Children in other classes watched out their windows, their faces pressed against the glass. They too were silent. Children have an odd sense of significance--and while they will often do or say the wrong thing in church or at the grocery store--they are quick to understand moments that go beyond their young comprehension.

The children gathered in a circle around the young tree that Larry had carried out and placed beside the hole. They were wearing winter parkas and heavy coats and some still wore their mittens and scarfs. As Mrs. Roberts began to unwrap the green burlap cover, wet and clumped with dirt, one by one the children began to kneel down beside her. They helped move the tree and push the dirt in around the thin white trunk.

"Let me pour in some dirt," one child said. Several others joined him until the hole was filled. Jane began to pat the dirt down with the palm of her hand, and all the children joined her. For several moments there was the silent thumping of little palms against the cold spring dirt.

When the tree was settled in the ground, the children backed up and looked away. Larry, towering above the gathering, picked up the shovel and stepped back from the tree awkwardly. The kids were unnaturally quiet. The only sound was their boots squishing in the first spring mud that had gathered in depressions on the fresh grass. The scent of cool grass and mud filled the air.

Gloria touched the new tree and said, "In a few weeks these buds will begin to swell and soon the tree will be covered with green leaves." The kids all looked at her, some nodding, but still unnaturally solemn. "And every time you look at this tree, you will remember Mr. Falise."

A cold breeze blew her blonde hair loose about her face. She wiped a tear back from her eye with a single finger and then gave a forced smile. "Come on. Let's go in now," she said.

As they walked back to their classroom, Gloria began singing softly a popular folk song. The words drifted back on the spring air.

"The answer, my friend, is blowing in the wind. The answer is blowing in the wind."

## Chapter 8
## A Peek Inside the Principal's Office

An elementary school principal often wakes up to the horrible shrill sound of a telephone. Bob's home was his office in the early hours of the morning. The calls were from sick teachers who needed a substitute for the day. Bob hated these calls. He cursed the district office for not having a central call system. He knew substitute teachers would be grateful for a central call system as well. It would end the many phone calls they would get in the morning after already accepting a teaching assignment.

Bob was sure most of the teachers who called were truly sick and probably deserved sympathy. But it took all the cheeriness he could muster at that time of morning to not sound grumpy. It took timing and strategy to find a good substitute teacher. It was like going to an auction. Good substitute were in demand and their phone might ring four or five times after they'd already agreed to substitute in another school. Usually their voices were as sleepy and grumpy as his at that hour. Bob was surprised one morning when the sub came to the telephone laughing.

"Mr. Kinsella, you have to hear this."

Her young son had answered the phone, she said, and came to the bedroom door with the standard, "Mom! Phone for you!"

## A Peek Inside the Principal's Office

"Who is it?" she asked, not wanting to get out of bed.

"Must be the principal," the boy replied with disgust, "Who else would want you?"

The school office was supposed to be a quiet place where the principal drafted the budget, wrote and rewrote schedules, wrote observation reports, prepared the weekly teacher's bulletin, prepared reports, reviewed testing material, prepared for meeting and caught up on the latest articles on education. The paperwork was important but the concerns of teachers, parents and children were the principal's first priority. Bob's office door was usually open to welcome visitors. If a deadline was looming, however, Bob did close the door with instruction to Alice not to interrupt.

Of course, sometime interruptions came anyhow. Bob clearly remembers one time when the door was closed. He heard a thumping noise in the outer office. An angry voice snarled, "Where's the principal?"

"He's busy now," Alice's pleasant voice answered. "May I help you?"

"No! He'd better see me and now, and he'd better do something about it too!"

"Would you like an appointment?" Alice's voice was still calm, but now it grew louder so that Bob could hear, "Mr. Wilson?"

Bob stood up immediately. Mr. Wilson was an angry man, difficult to work with, and it wasn't fair to leave Alice to cope with him on her own. Opening the door, Bob saw Alice backing toward his office, her arms outstretched to prevent Mr. Wilson from bursting in and her legs moving to avoid the heavy thumps of his cane. He was a wiry man, dressed in work clothes that smelled of sweat and stale beer.

"Come in, Mr. Wilson," Bob said loudly. Alice gave him a furtive look of thanks as she ducked around the angry, cane-waving man and went back to her desk.

"Good thing for you, you're seeing me," Mr. Wilson growled as he stomped into the office, "I was going to make you a lotta trouble."

Bob listened patiently to Mr. Wilson's ranting. He accused a bus driver of hitting his son Danny. He claimed he had actually seen the bus driver hitting the boy. Then Mr. Wilson stormed out of the office with a parting comment, "You better take care of this!"

Bob knew the story wasn't true. Mr. Wilson kept referring to the bus driver as a man, and the bus driver of that route was a woman, as most of our bus drivers were. Bob called Chuckie, the oldest son in the family, down to his office to get the real story.

Chuckie spoke up without hesitation. What happened is that Danny wet his pants on the bus and was worried that the school nurse would call home about it. So he made up the story about the bus driver hitting him. If you knew the family, this sort of lying to shift the blame made complete sense. The family dynamics were frustrating, and there was little Bob could do about it. He decided to just ignore the incident for the time being, knowing that next time he saw Mr. Wilson he would have something new to be angry about.

Students often appear in the principal's office with a note from a teacher, often a note that indicated that the teacher wanted the student punished. The note might say that the child was talking, or couldn't sit in his seat, or he was disrupting class, that he was swearing or stealing, or that he hadn't done his homework. Some teachers used the principal as the ultimate threat while others just wanted Bob to keep them in the office till they calmed down. Often the infractions were minor, and often Bob's biggest challenge was keeping a straight face as he dealt with the problems.

One time, four boys from one class were sent to the office with a note that read: "These four boys were rude and insolent during reading class."

Bob gave them a stern lecture on behavior. All four boys hung their heads and admitted that yes, they had been rude and insolent. At the end of his lecture, Bob asked emphatically, "Is that clear?"

They all nodded meekly. Matt raised his hand and asked a bit timidly, "What do you mean by rude and insolent—is that like kicking someone?"

Another time three boys were sent to the office for taking a boy's hat and putting it up out of his reach on a fence. It was a minor incident. When questioned why, they all agreed that they were mad at the boy for calling them names.

Bob gave the boys one of his disgusted looks and said, "I'm sure you call him names too." The boys protested. "No, we don't." Then one of the boys blurted out in frustration, "I can't think of anything to call him."

Another time, Bob spotted Jeff, a fourth grader, walking down the hall. He slowed down and kept looking down at his sneakers. He had a note in his hand.

"Is that for me?" Bob asked. The boy nodded.

Bob took the note and read it as they walked down the hall. It was from his teacher, "Jeff has been using swear words and I would appreciate it if you would talk to him about it. I'm afraid other parents will be upset about it."

Jeff readily admitted he did swear. Bob knew that children often learned the language from their parents, and he had to deal with these incidents carefully. He wanted to let Jeff know that swearing was not acceptable in the classroom, but he did not want to criticize his parents, who probably used that kind of language. Bob explained to Jeff that other parents didn't want their kids to swear or hear other children swear. "Jeff, I really don't care if you swear at home, but if you ever do it again at school, I'll

## A Peek Inside the Principal's Office

have to punish you." Jeff nodded, and Bob was sure he understood.

The next day Jeff's dad called. "Was Jeff in your office yesterday for swearing in school?"

Bob expected to hear a tirade about how he was wrong and that if the child was swearing, he must have learned it in our school. Then Jeff's father asked, "Did you tell him that he could swear at home?"

"Yes, but..."

Jeff's father interrupted the explanation with laughter. That evening at the dinner table, Jeff had looked at his mother and said, "Pass me the goddamned potatoes." His mother was horrified. But Jeff just looked at her and said, "Mr. Kinsella said it was all right to swear at home."

"Honestly," his father said, "we don't allow him to swear at home. His mother and I talked to him, and I'm sure that will be the last of it."

Another time, a fifth grade teacher sent Ivan to the office. One of the boys found his lost cards in Ivan's desk and another boy, Robert Taylor, said Ivan was wearing his lost sneakers. Ivan acted mystified by the appearance of the cards in his desk and he insisted that the sneakers were his. Knowing Ivan would stick to his story, Bob asked, "Do you know what initials are written inside the sneaks?"

Ivan looked surprised and raised his head. "RT?"

"Those are Roberts Taylor's initials."

"I know. I lost my sneaks and needed another pair--but I swear I didn't take those cards."

Bob sent him to sit quietly in the outer office to think about what he had done and what should be done about it. An hour later he told Alice he was sorry and felt bad about what he did.

Bob asked, "Why is it you feel bad, Ivan?"

"Cause I got caught!"

Another time a teacher sent a child to the office with his spelling paper. He misspelled 10 of the 20 spelling words. Surprisingly he spelled geography correctly, even though it was the most difficult word on the test. When Bob asked him how he knew how to spell geography, he said, "That is an easy one. Our teacher taught us a way to remember it. All we had to do was remember the first letters of the saying, "George Eaton's old grandmother rode a pig home yesterday."

Before and after school, and especially during lunchtime, teachers often showed up in the office, with suggestions, problems, and stories.

Bob can remember the time Norma came to his office just after school closed. She had a parent in tow. Her lips were pursed tightly and her black hair fell into her face. He could tell she was angry by the way she slapped a paper down on my desk. "This parent doesn't like the way I grade spelling tests!"

"I didn't say that," objected the parent.

The parent was an attractive woman who seemed a bit out of breath. It was obvious the two women had walked from the classroom to Bob's office at a pretty fast pace. Her daughter Pam, new to our school, was a shy little girl with big eyes and strawberry blond curls. "I was just asking her why my daughter got such a low grade on her spelling test when the words are all spelled correctly."

Bob picked up Pam's test and skimmed over it. All the words were spelled correctly. However, the child had used capital letters in place of small ones for some letters, and Norma had marked those words wrong.

Bob looked across at Pam's mom and said, "I understand your position. The words are all spelled correctly." She smiled. Before Norma had time to cut in, he turned and looked into her angry eyes. "I understand your position too, Norma. I know how you teach, and am certain that before the test, you warned the children that if they used capital letters in place of small letters, the word would be marked wrong."

Turning the spelling test so that they could both look at it, Bob said, "I think that the grade on the paper should remain since the other students in the class had words marked wrong for the same problem."

Bob asked Norma to take time to go over the test with Pam and explain why she got the words marked wrong. Norma nodded and seemed to be simmering down. She probably didn't expect support for her position.

He asked Pam's mother if she would practice at home with Pam on writing small letters. She nodded yes. As Bob got the two of them talking about ways to help the child, they both seemed to calm down, but he couldn't help but think the whole incident was a terrible introduction to the school. A different teacher could have settled the whole issue herself without rancor.

Another time, a fourth grade teacher, a sweet older woman, appeared in Bob's office with a boy in tow. "I caught Donny with some nasty cards. He passed the cards to all the children in my math class."

Her voice was hushed and her face a bright crimson. "I thought you had better know before the parents start calling." She then gave Bob a manila envelope, sealed tightly and reinforced with layers and layers of masking tape and said, "The cards are inside."

Bob could picture the scene. The students had just come into the room for their math lesson. Donny, with a serious, helpful look on his round little face, marched up and down the rows, passing one card to each child. Silence fell over the room as the children looked down at the cards, then up at the teacher, then down at the cards again in open-mouthed surprise. No one said a word. The teacher began class as usual, but couldn't get the children's attention. Finally the teacher glanced down at one of the cards and nearly fainted.

Bob unraveled the layers of tape, took out a set of porno cards, and asked, "Where did you get these?"

"My father had them behind the bar." Donny's calm pose vanished for a moment, "Don't call Dad. We're not supposed to play with his cards."

In a stern voice, Bob told Donny what he already knew -- that he shouldn't have those cards in school and certainly shouldn't have passed them out to the children in the math class. Bob told him to tell his dad tonight and have him call in the morning otherwise he would call him.

The next day Donny's dad strode into the principal's office. "Mr. Kinsella," he began, "Donny told me about the porno cards and I was horrified. May I see the cards?" Reaching into the center drawer, Bob took out the cards. After examining them, Donny's father smacked his clenched fist into his other hand and with a self-righteous air, "If I ever catch the guy who gave those cards to my kid, he'll regret it."

He handed the cards back to Bob, who stuck them in his shirt pocket.

Bob shook his head in disgust and said, "Donny told me that he got the cards from behind your bar." The father mumbled something and left quickly. Bob considered the incident over. In fact, he forgot all about the cards, which were still in his shirt pocket.

Later that day, in the dentist's office, he ran into a parent also there for a dental appointment. Always ready to talk to a parent, Bob closed his magazine and leaned over to put it back into the floor rack. As he did so, the porno cards slipped from his pocket and scattered across the floor.

The mother turned to help pick up the cards. She reached for the nearest card and then her hand froze at the sight of nude bodies on the faces of the cards. "I guess you don't need my help picking these up," she said icily.

"No, wait. These aren't mine." He began frantically picking up every card in sight. Why had so many landed right side up?

"I took these from a student today," he said, his face turning red.

"I see," she said. But it took several minutes of stammering explanations before Bob could get her to understand what had actually happened.

Most of Bob's teachers had a sense of humor about the fairly innocent mischief that went on in school and were quick to tell him stories. One teacher was doing playground duty, when a boy ran up to her and reported that a kid named Matt had a picture of a naked woman. As the teacher walked over to the cluster of giggling boys, she saw Matt give Ernie a ripped piece of paper. Ernie folded it

## A Peek Inside the Principal's Office

and stuffed it in his pockets as the teacher approached.

"Hey, Ernie," the teacher asked, "What've you got there?"

Ernie's face turned red. He stammered. "I only got a leg."

Another teacher told about a little boy during show-and-tell time displaying his new t-shirt. He untucked the shirt from his pants so that the class could see it clearly.

"It is real nice and white," the teacher said admiringly.

"Yes," the boy nodded, "and it goes way down below my peter."

Another teacher told about how his class returned from music class very excited. They were all chattering about how their music teacher had scolded Donny and Ralph. The teacher asked, "Why did you get scolded?" Neither boy answered. The room was silent as the teacher waited.

Finally a loud voice in the back yelled out, "Them were farting around."

A third grade teacher gave me a note she had taken from a girl named Jennifer while she was monitoring a math test:

"Dear Rickey, I love you very much. Di you love me yes or no. I will chesy you out siade. Will you kiss me?"

After the teacher took the note, Jennifer looked at her and asked, "Why are you always around at the wrong time?"

A fifth grade teacher came to Bob's office several times complaining about a child that got off a bus at school and waited to be picked up by another bus to take him to his special class. He didn't want him coming to his room anymore. Bob didn't see it as a problem and ignored it. Actually, he felt the teacher was wrong to even ask. The teacher stopped again after school and again asked to have the boy stop getting off the bus and going to his room. Disgusted, Bob told him he didn't see anything wrong with the boy waiting in his room for the bus and he wouldn't stop it.

Angrily the teacher said, "You would if he came into your room every day and piddled on your wall!"

A first grade teacher told about the time she put shy seven-year-old Dora in charge of her class and sent them to the library. She went back into the classroom and began putting up a bulletin board. When she looked out in the hall, she noticed that the class hadn't left. "Now class," little Dora was saying in clear tones, "If this line isn't straight, and you don't stop talking, we aren't moving".

A kindergartener knew all the hot buttons to push to set his teacher off. She often sent him to the office with a note that read, "Billy can't sit still! He is constantly talking and bothering other students. He rarely ever does any school work!" Exasperated with him, she scheduled a parent conference and wanted the principal present. The parents listened as the teacher started reciting the many things Billy did to cause trouble in her class. The father interrupted her and said, "If you would stop coddling him and just give him a whack on his backside he would behave. That's what I do, and it takes care of his nonsense." Although not happy with the idea of paddling a kindergarten child, Bob did agreed to do as the father requested

The district policy was that only the principal could exercise corporal punishment and then only with a witness present. Alice was the witness and she hated the duty. Fortunately this policy was later changed, ending corporal punishment.

Early the next morning, Billy appeared in the office with the normal note. He was told to put his hands on his desk and to bend over. Bob gave him a whack on his backside with a yardstick and sent him back to class. That afternoon he was again in the office and got another whack. The next morning he walked into the office, put his hands on the desk, bent over and waited to be whacked with the yardstick. Bob looked at the little guy and could see a boy determined not to let the principal see him cry. Instead of paddling him, he had him sit in a chair. He looked so small and innocent in the big orange chair. Bob got out of his chair and walked toward him. He could see the boy's body get rigid, ready for a real beating. Instead, Bob sat down in the chair next to him, put his arm around him and pulled him close to him and said, "Billy, I'm sorry.

I promise you that as long as I am principal, you will never again get paddled in school."

Billy nestled a little closer to his principal and it almost looked like a tear was forming. He never became a good student and he continued to be sent to the office for his behavior but now instead of being paddled he got time out. After a brief talk about his behavior, he was sent to Alice's office to sit at an extra table in her room. She always made sure the table was stocked with paper and crayons. He would sit quietly, drawing until it was time to return to class. Alice enjoyed Billy and the feeling was mutual. He was always a model student in her presence.

Bob saw his share of parents in the office too. Many came with concerns about their children, or PTO matters. Some were angry, while others wanted to share a cute story. Bob always encouraged parents to stop in the office at any time to share a funny or cute story about their children, and many did. Often the story was a way for shy but concerned parents to talk to the principal about ideas and problems.

Whenever Bob came in first thing in the morning and saw a woman sitting silently in the outer office, he always knew what to expect. Quietly, he would ask Alice to clear his schedule, as he handled the morning routines, getting kids off the buses and into the classrooms, before approaching the woman. He knew exactly what she was going to say, "My husband just left me."

Bob referred to these incidents as "Morning Syndrome." Charlotte was one of these women. She was a warm fun person to be with. Her husband was an accountant with a large firm in the city. Charlotte never worked outside the home and was an active member of the PTO. She was always available to help on school projects.

Charlotte was always late for PTO meetings. It was fun to watch her try to slip in quietly. Her bouncy walk and full head of blonde hair that hung loose to her waist was hard to miss.

Charlotte came into the office, sat down in a chair and began talking. "I don't know how to tell you this, Mr. Kinsella. . . I'm sorry to even have to bother you with this. . ." Her voice quivered. "But I think it is important for the children's sake that I do." She reached into her purse and began rummaging through it while she spoke. "Last night, my husband left me. It was all of a sudden. He came home and started packing his clothes and. . . I had no idea he'd leave. Honestly, I didn't know." She pulled a tissue from her purse and wiped her eyes. They were now red and puffy. Sitting in the big chair, twisting a strand of hair around her finger, she looked about twelve years old. Tears streamed down her face.

"I had no idea he would leave. Honestly. I didn't know." She wiped her eyes, put the tissue on her lap, and folded her hands in an attempt to regain composure. "I don't know what to do. I'm not sure how to handle my kids. They're so hurt. Julie cried all last night. They love their Dad so. He took them out to pick apples last weekend. We all started throwing rotten apples--it was. . . I mean, I never. . . I just can't. . ."

"I didn't know it was going to happen. I didn't even know he was seeing her. She got transferred to New Jersey and he's going with her." She tried to laugh through her tears but it only made her cry harder. "I met her once at their yearly Christmas party. I never even suspected. I must be pretty stupid. Other people knew. His boss--he knew. But the kids, of course, they didn't know. I still don't think they understand. I just don't know what to do for the kids. What should I do?"

Charlotte was acting just like the wonderful mother she was. Even while her marriage was falling apart she was thinking about what was best for her children. She was worried sick about them, afraid what this might do to them. Yet she didn't insult or criticize her husband--didn't say a single bad word about him.

"What are you doing for money?"

"I don't need anything from my husband. I can take care of my kids by myself."

"Do you have a lawyer?"

"Yes. I haven't talked to him since we did our wills last year."

"You should call him today. You need to know what your rights are--and the rights of your children and your responsibilities."

She nodded. "I'll do whatever I can for my kids."

Bob tried to reassure her: "I'll talk to Julie's teacher--and John's too. We'll keep a close eye on them. If there are any changes in academic progress or social behavior, we'll let you know."

Bob felt it was important for the school to respond to the needs of these families. Teachers needed to be alert to changes in behavior or grades of these children and together with parents try helping them in this time of need. School had to be seen as a safe, understanding place for children.

Other sad situations were less typical. Bob knew one family that consisted of five kids, four boys and a girl, who lived with their father at the edge of town. He was an uneducated, hard-working man who did the best he could to bring up his children. They were good kids--a shy, well-mannered group. Lisa, the oldest, was a quiet little girl whose maternal instincts were evident in the way that she looked after her younger brothers. Bob often saw her with the boys at the breakfast program in the mornings. It was cute the way she tucked in Tony's shirt or handed Dennis some Kleenex to stuff in his pocket.

Late one afternoon, a woman appeared in Bob's office, claiming to be the mother of the five kids. Bob was startled. He knew the family hadn't seen her since little Tony was a baby. She was a small, dark-haired woman whose blue eye make-up caught the glare of the overhead lights in the office. Next to her stood a huge, hairy man. His left arm was decorated with several tattoos, the homemade India-ink-under-the-skin variety.

"I am here to get my children," She spoke quietly and precisely, like a schoolgirl reciting a practiced speech. "I have legal custody of them. I've missed them over the years. Now that I'm married again, they are coming with me."

Bob looked at her in surprise and she kept talking, "Lisa will stay--she can go on living with her father--but I'll take the boys. We are leaving this afternoon so they will have to come with me now. I have the papers right here."

Bob looked over the papers and noted that legal custody of the children had been awarded to her over five years ago.

"What are we waiting for?" She stood up, snapping her purse shut. "You've seen the papers."

Bob stood up and emphatically said, "Those children came here on a school bus, and they will go home on the school bus." The two looked at him in disgust, but left the office. Bob called the father of the children and told him the story. He then called Fred, our police chief and encouraged him to be there when the bus arrives at the home.

Monday morning, Lisa came to school alone. She went quietly to her classroom. She never said a word about what happened. Later we heard from a school up north telling us that the children were enrolled in their school. We never heard anything of those boys again.

Bob's home phone number was listed in the phone book, and he did get some calls at night about school matters. A few were serious but most just wanted information. Sometimes, though, the caller was an angry parent talking in aggressive tone. Bob would move the receiver far from his ear and listen. He was used to these calls. Just like the mothers who sat in his office early in the morning were referred to as Early Morning Syndrome--the night calls became known as Evening Syndrome. The calls always came between 6 and 8 PM and always involved a shouting parent. The parent could just as easily have waited until morning to call. But they wanted to prove to their child that school did not intimidate them. Bob knew the child was standing nearby listening. And he suspected that these parents had once been children who had bad experience in school.

Bob would listen as the father screamed and ranted.

Then when he paused to catch his breath, Bob would ask quietly, "Could you have your child leave the room?"

The silence on the other end usually told Bob that he had surprised the parent. Then usually, he would hear the father ask the child to leave the room. Once the child had left the room, Bob was often able to talk to the parent in a more reasonable way.

Bob still remembers his very first time in the principal's office where he spent so many years. He was being interviewed for the job. During the interview, he noticed that Doug, the retiring principal, was limping from what appeared to be a very recent injury. At the very end of the session, Doug apologized for not giving Bob a walk around the school. He hesitated at first to explain why, and then said, "Oh, what the hell, I might as well tell you this story."

That morning Doug got a call from an agitated first grade teacher, "Mr. Zoller, Donny's throwing stones at kids on the playground."

Worried that someone was going to get hurt, Doug hurried to the playground. Fortunately Donny's aim was poor. And soon as Donny saw the principal he took off running. Doug chased him around the slide, through the barber-pole painted swings, and under the jungle gym. Doug's long legs finally let him catch Donny at the crabapple tree just before he got to the driveway. He swooped Donny up in his right arm, pressed him against his hip and headed confidently to the office with his prize. As he walked toward the door, Donny reached down between Doug's legs and grabbed him in a very sensitive spot.

"Owww! Let go before I wallop you!" Doug yelled.

In a very small voice, Donny said, "You first."

Doug was still wincing as he told the story. "The thing that makes me most angry was that he won."

Perhaps in respect for Doug's pain, Bob should have tried to keep a straight face and say something sympathetic, but instead he roared with laughter. And Doug laughed too. An appropriate beginning to the many years Bob would spend in the principal's office.

## Chapter 9
## Snow Flakes and Sleigh Bells

Christmas trees began appearing in classroom in early December -- real trees, that arrived dripping with wet snow, filling the classroom with the scent of pine. Some trees were pretty scrawny, while others would fill an entire corner. Nowadays, schools are limited to artificial trees, but plastic trees out of a box cannot possibly match the excitement a real tree brings.

The classroom tree project often began with the teacher asking, "Who thinks their parent can bring us a tree?" Every hand in the room would go up. Every child believed that his or her family would be able to get a tree for the classroom. The first family to send in a note saying that they could get a tree would be the ones to provide the tree.

Janine can still remember the excitement in the classroom the day the tree would arrive. The teacher would not mention the tree; she would be trying to run class as usual, getting the children to work on math problems or reading. But the kid whose Dad was bringing in the tree would be bursting to tell his friends, and soon the whole classroom would be whispering, "The tree is coming today." The skinny kid who sat in the row over the window would wait until the teacher's back was turned and sneak over to look out the window. "I think I saw his truck go by!"

After many false alarms, suddenly there'd be a knock on the door. At that point, even the quietest kids in the classroom would give up the pretense of doing their work. The door would burst open, and someone's Dad, dressed in work clothes and big boots, with a big grin on his face, would stomp into the room, laughing and shaking snow all over the floor, dragging in a big pine tree. Every child watched while he pulled it into the corner and lifted the big tree into the stand without any effort at all. The teacher would be thanking the father, and talking nicely to him, but the kids wouldn't say a word at this point. They would just be looking at the tree, and then at each other, smiling the whole time, and the kid whose Dad had just come in would be nearly bursting with pride.

Eventually, the Dad would leave, usually after giving a shy glance at the class and a wink at his son and a smile to some of the kids in the class he knew. The teacher would say something exasperating like, "Now, we can't decorate the tree today because we have to let the snow melt." But the rest of the day, the scent of pine filled the room, and every child would look up from their math sheet after every single problem to check on the tree and admire how nice it looked.

Most of the trees did not come from Christmas tree farms but had been cut in the woods or a field. Dorothy Ford, one of our kindergarten teachers, had many years of experience trying to help five-year-olds decorate trees that were either way too skinny or so full that they had no shape. She said to Bob cheerfully, "The worse the tree looked at the beginning, the better it looked after the children finish decorating it." She paused, and added: "Sometimes it is truly a creative challenge."

The appearance of Christmas trees in the classrooms and red and green paper chains in the halls was accompanied by the sound of children practicing Christmas songs. Most of our students were just learning to play. Bob would often wince as he heard the painful shriek of a clarinet coming from the instrumental music room. Sometimes it sounded like the child was fighting with the instrument. Bob often wondered how Dick, the music teacher, could stand the noise. He himself was often tempted to rush into the room and rescue the poor clarinet from the child's hand. But the sound would stop, the door would open, and Dick would be cheerfully saying, "Good work" to the small child carrying the clarinet case. Sometimes, he would turn to say hello to Bob.

"Hi Bob, are you listening to the sweet sounds of the wind instruments?"

"How can you stand that noise all day?"

He would laugh: "Bob, that may be noise to others--but to me it's the start of music. I'll shape those sounds, teaching them to loosen or tighten their lips. And eventually we'll make beautiful music--just in time for the Christmas concert."

"You'd probably laugh seeing me make faces to show the kids the proper way to blow the instrument. Most kids start by puffing out their cheeks. The air goes right from their lungs and into the cheeks and not a puff makes it into the instrument. But with time they learn how to play."

As they talked, students were at the door with their trumpets. They carried big cases for the instruments that looked like luggage in their small hands. They seemed anxious to begin their lesson. Dick closed the door and soon the brash almost bossy sound of trumpets in the hands of young children filled the hallway.

Another Christmas tradition in our school was the canned good drive for needy families. One year a new twist was added to the drive. The class with the longest trail of canned goods would win an ice cream treat. The students loved the idea. Soon, even the smallest kindergartener was lugging cans of vegetables or fruit from the bus into their classroom. The can food trails snaked around the tiled floors of every classroom and in a few classes they went out into the halls. Bob wondered about the wisdom of the plan every time he tripped over a line of canned goods, but the students so loved the idea that it became a tradition.

Every morning during this time of year, Bob would see children clustered around the Christmas box. A large, brightly decorated box with a slit on the top, it stood in the main hallway waiting for letters from children for Santa. A big sign read: "Letters to Santa." The front of the box had a decorative drawing of Santa with a bag full of presents thrown over his shoulder.

The first year we set up the box, the children stuffed any paper containing their list in the slot, usually signing only their first names to the letter. We had hoped the staff would be able to respond to each child's letter--but we discovered it was impossible since we couldn't tell which Bobby or Mike or Jennifer wrote the letter. We thought we would have many disappointed children that first year, until the art teacher, came up with a solution. She posted Santa's reply over the box on large poster paper. She wrote using big letters and addressed the reply with the names of all the children who had dropped letters in the box.

*Dear Mike, Bobby, Dave, Jennifer, Mary etc.*

*Thank you for writing. Some of my elves got sick this year so I'm busy making toys. I can't answer each of your letters this year but please write again next year and I promise I'll write to each of you.*

*Love,*
*Santa*

After the near disaster the first year, teachers handed out special sheets of paper to each child with the class name written on the top. The children used this paper to write to Santa. Their teachers encouraged them to use both their first and last name so that Santa would know they worked hard in school and could write their full name. The children thought this was a great idea and most did as instructed. Every night the box was emptied and delivered to high school students who answered the letters and had them returned to each child. Some of the children still used only their first names. Knowing the classroom of these children, even with more than one child in the class with the same name, only a little detective work was required. Usually this involved the teachers asking the children what they wanted and then, correlated with their wish list, were able to know who wrote the letter. Children would squeal when they opened their letter.

"Look!" the child would shout. "Santa answered my letter." One of the high school students said the letter her little brother received was the most unbelievable thing that ever happened to him. Her brother only got one or two presents from his list but he kept saying, "Imagine Santa knowing exactly what I wanted and then getting it for me."

The letter written by John made us cry. John was Charlotte's youngest. Her husband had walked out on her. He only had one item on his list: "Please Santa send Daddy home. I love him."

Teachers even got into the spirit. Sam was an athletic boy whose father was a huge, powerful man who worked on the railroad. Concerned that his dad wouldn't get Sam the one present he wanted, she wrote the father a letter.

*Dear Mr. Logan,*

*Santa asked me to write you a note. He said that he ran out of teddy bears this year but knows that Sam really wants a bear. In fact a teddy bear is the only thing Sam put on his list. Sam has been a good boy all year. Please buy him a teddy bear for me.*

*Sincerely,*

*Sam's teacher*
*and Santa's helper*

Bob was surprised to see Sam, who had the reputation of being a tough kid, come in the day after Christmas vacation, proudly clutching a teddy bear.

One evening during December, families gathered in the cafeteria for the annual school musical and play. The children were always anxious to show off their talents to their parents. The girls were often excited to arrive wearing their Christmas dresses, often red velvet, with matching red bows in their hair. The boys were less thrilled to be forced into their Sunday clothes. The traditional pose for a boy standing in line would be to pull his tie sideways and up, make a face, and say, "I am choking to death." We always had a whole group of toddlers who would wander up near the stage, often just as entertaining as what was happening on the stage.

The children in the audience would mouth the words to the songs, clapping and tapping their feet to the music. Gone were the high-pitched squeaks and squawks; the kids could play recognizable songs. The clarinets, trumpets, and trombones were strong and clear, and the sounds of drums beating on a rubber pad were replaced by the jazzy sound of a snare drum. Parents often joked that after listening to the noise of their children practicing at home that it was unbelievable to them that music actually would come out of those instruments.

A mother, on her way to her car with her child, told how excited she was by the performance. "What a wonderful play," she said. "My daughter had a temperature of 102 but she insisted on coming." Her daughter smiled up at her and they walked out together. The girl's role in the play was a Christmas tree. She had two lines.

Another child named Gary was in line to go on stage when he realized he had left his clarinet back in the music room. He raced back to the room, grabbed his instrument, and arrived on stage just in time to begin playing. Since he was completely out of breath from running, all the high notes came with a whistle. After the performance he came up to the music teacher and said, "I'm all through with show business."

The last day before Christmas, kids came to school filled with excitement, many of them clutching gifts for their teachers and a bag of candy to share with the class. Right after school opened, we gathered the kindergarten, first, and second grade children in the cafeteria for a breakfast sponsored by the PTO. The children would be quiet at first, eating and looking around with big eyes while a teacher played a Christmas movie.

When Bob would look out his window and see a police car pull into the circle, he would know that Santa had arrived. Fred, the Minoa police chief, had been playing Santa Claus for years. He was a large man who needed no padding in his red suit. He had a ruddy complexion to complement his beard and suit, and the children always took to him immediately and laughed at all his jokes. He'd come into the cafeteria in full costume, a big bag slung over his back.

One time, just after Fred left the elementary school after Santa's Breakfast, a call came over his car radio. There had been an accident on Main Street. He hurried over to check the injured driver. The man looked up from his car, saw the police chief in his costume, and asked in disbelief, "Santa, what are you doing here?"

Fred threatened to quit as our Santa after that incident, but of course he didn't. He loved to play the part. He would stand just outside the door to the cafeteria and shake a long string of bells. At the sound, the kids would all stop talking and look up. "It's Santa!" some of them would cry. "He's here!" They'd all stand up to get the first look.

The little children screamed when they saw him. "Hello Santa!" or "It really is Santa!" Some of the little ones just stared in awe.

When Santa reached the center of the stage, he placed a finger to his mouth. Immediately the children were quiet. He took a seat in an overstuffed chair. The teachers lined the children up, and one by one they talked to Santa. They asked questions when they reached him, and some couldn't resist hugging him. Others, however, stood back, afraid to get near him. Brad, the class clown, turned on all his charm, climbed on his lap, and announce in a loud voice, "I love you Santa!"

Each child received a candy cane and a letter from Santa. The letter was rolled and tied with a tiny ribbon. It was a beautiful letter, telling the children about his workshop in the North Pole and saying how he was looking forward to seeing them this Christmas. Santa got out of his chair and walked around the cafeteria talking to the children-- especially the quiet shy ones. Children hugged and kissed him as he bent over their table. Most were happy just to touch him. One Child asked, "Where's Rudolph?" When Fred pointed across the road, he set off a flurry of excitement. "I see Rudolph!" a child shouted. And soon all the children could see Santa's reindeer and his sled across the street.

At the end of the visit Santa stood by the door and said good-bye to the children as they left for their rooms. Bob walked Fred to the front lobby and thanked him again and whispered, "Don't forget to take off your suit this year."

That afternoon, classrooms had their parties. Children were responsible for bringing in certain items. Some brought in cookies or cupcakes, others juice or soda or candy. Each of the children also brought in a gift for the traditional gift exchange. As a school policy, we set a maximum price of 50 cents for the gift. Surprisingly the reason for a maximum price for gifts was that children that could least afford it bought the most expensive gifts. It helped end some nasty comments like:

"I don't like this gift."

"I gave a better gift then this."

Sometimes we would even get parents calling to complain that the gift they gave was more expensive than the gift their child received. The price limit helped stopped that.

Teachers always got presents. Their gifts were usually quite predictable--Avon products, gaudy jewelry, handicrafts, cologne, Christmas ornaments, and always lifesavers. Of course there were the unusual gifts. One teacher received a large wreath of turkey feathers. As she thanked the child, she sneezed; she was allergic to feathers.

Some children didn't bring any presents for their teacher. They would say, "I'm going to buy your present tomorrow" or "I was going to buy your present last night but my Mom made me go to bed early."

Bob visited all the classes laughing with the kids and talking with them about what they wanted for Christmas. They ate cookies and drank soda and played the special games the teachers had prepared for them. Each classroom party was different, depending on the personalities of the teacher and the room mothers. In one room, the desks would be pushed back and the kids would be playing a lively game in the middle of the room. In another room, the kids would have the desks pushed together like tables and they would be quietly talking, eating, or playing cards.

Near the end of the parties the classes took down the decorations and put away the Christmas ornaments. The trees were placed in the parking lot, laid neatly on the ground for any family who needed a tree. By Christmas Eve, most trees were gone.

When the school day finally ended, the children boarded their buses for home. Exhausted, the staff would gather in small groups, talking and laughing. The teachers packed up their strange assortment of presents and finished cleaning their classrooms. Many were heading home now to prepare for the holidays – cleaning, cooking, traveling. Despite the busyness, everyone was in a festive mood as they yelled across the snowy parking lot: "See you next year!"

## Chapter 10
## Flunking Out

Jerry was a chubby little boy with big dark eyes who always wanted to please. He was held back in first grade because he wasn't reading at grade level. The next year the teacher asked her first grade class what they wanted to be when they grew up. Many gave the standard answers: policeman, firefighter, teacher, football player, doctor, and astronaut. When she asked Jerry, he said, "A clown."

"Why would you be a clown?" the teacher asked curiously.

The little boy said simply: "Because everyone laughs at me."

The concept of social promotion was a hot topic in the late 70's and early 80's. Many thought children like Jerry would profit from repeating a grade. Many educators and parents believed that performance of students would improve if schools established standards and insisted that kids meet them before moving on to the next grade.

Bob's school board decided to study the benefits and drawbacks of social promotion in their district. The head of the testing department developed a position paper stating that children in first grade who were reading below grade level should be retained. She felt that if the children were retained in first grade, they would be able to continue through the rest of their school life reading at grade level.

Many educators applauded this position. Bob worried that the institution of this policy would only put fear and excessive pressure on the students who were in no danger of failing. The threat of failure often raised the average test scores in a class, which at first indicated that retention was a successful strategy. The fear of failure puts extra pressure on the top students in the class, and the middle range of students as well, sometimes pushing their test scores higher. The policy had little effect on failing students, who know they were failing and had already given up. Bob worried about a policy that did not help this group of students.

Education researcher Don Moore stated: "It's unethical, if you know that retention is harmful to knowingly harm one group of students in order to benefit another. Which parent wants their child retained and have their life ruined in order to motivate the child beside him to work harder?"

When the school board learned that about 30% of first graders would fail and many of these students were from prominent families in the community, they decided to rethink their position. They hired two respected professors from the School of Education at Syracuse University, Dr. Sheldon and Dr.Glennon, as consultants to review the plan. After reviewing sound, carefully structured research on retention from the 1930s to the 1980s, they reported their finding to the school board. The report clearly showed that retaining students failed to improve performance and that children retained rarely caught up to grade level in reading. Their research was so convincing that the Board changed the policy to read: "Retention should only be used in rare cases and then only as a last resort."

Bob was still concerned. He knew that retention was a simplistic solution that didn't help the failing child. He was pleased, however, that children wouldn't be routinely failed because they were reading below grade level. It was clear to him that holding a child back a grade, separating him from his friends, making him feel like a failure, and forcing him to go over the same workbook sheets that didn't teach him anything the first time was not the answer. But he also knew that social promotion – just passing kids along wasn't the answer either. He knew that the main reason children were held back a grade was because they weren't reading at grade level.

In Bob's school district reading instruction started in kindergarten. Children were tested in the summer and placed into reading groups. The top group started in the fall, the next group in December and slowest group would start in the spring. The goal of the program was to move the children through the reading program as quickly as possible as a way to challenging students ready for reading instruction. The philosophy of the program is that the more skills the child acquires, the more the child will want to read.

A major problem with this procedure was that it created a caste system within the classroom – children learned quickly whether they were in the smart group or the dummy group and they acted accordingly. A child not ready to learn to read at the age of five was put into the lowest group and found it difficult to ever catch up to their classmates regardless of their ability. The system especially penalized boys, who as a group lag behind girls in language development.

The most important factor in a child's reading success is how often the child reads. Schools need to stress reading and books must permeate the classroom. If schools want an alternative to simply failing students, they need to devise ways to get the children reading more. Parents and teachers need to work together to encourage children to read, to awaken their curiosity in books.

One of the most important thing a parent or teacher can do is encourage children to read for pleasure. As a sixth grade teacher, Janine always had a book to read aloud to her students so that any dead time could be taken up with reading. She read aloud to the students at the end of the day when they were gathering their books together and getting their coats. The kids loved being read to so much they would be as quiet as could be as they got ready to go home; the reading made the end of the day very peaceful and enjoyable.

Janine also gave the children chances to read aloud to each other. If learning centers are set up within the classroom, children can have opportunities to read to each other. They can do things like write and illustrate their own books. Learning to read can be fun and silly – like putting nouns on post-it notes and putting them on the objects they name. Teaching a child to read is about arousing a child's curiosity, about nurturing that child's inquisitiveness. If a child loves to read, he will be a good reader.

Most school use a basal reader series that is developed for each grade level. These books are filled with great stories with guides that help children learn to read. Yet teachers also know that for children to become good readers, they need to develop a love for reading. These short stories are a start but children must read for pleasure, to see books as fun and exciting and interesting, to realize that books can take them places and teach them things. To do this books must permeate the school, teachers must read to kids, kids should read to other kids, and parents must be involved. The trick is to get children to want to read, so that they are reading on weekends, evenings, and most importantly, over summer vacation.

Today, many children are not readers simply because they don't have time to read. Television, computer games, sports, and other organized activities take up much of a child's day. Schools cannot solve this problem without parent involvement. The axiom that the more a child reads, even comic books and sport magazines, the better reader he will become is true.

An important way parents can help their child learn to read is to make sure the television and computer screen stay blank for long periods of time so the children will get bored and turn to books. A child needs time to get bored. When a child gets bored enough, books will become appealing. Even an adult waiting in a doctor's office will read any magazine while they wait.

Janine's method of turning her own children into readers would probably seem extreme to many parents. At the beginning of summer vacation, she unplugged her television set and puts it in the garage until the end of summer vacation.

Reading and writing are closely intertwined. Both support the other. When Janine taught creative writing in the elementary schools, she discovered that some of the students were so worried about neatness that they end up paralyzed as writers. She often showed them her own journals from elementary school, filled with cross-outs and doodles, sometimes even words written sideways or upside down, and explained that a journal is a place for messy writing. Neatness matters when you are writing a formal essay for a teacher, but children also need to learn how to express their ideas in a way that is more creative and experimental. The messy journal is a place where kids can write because it feels good. And like reading, the more you write the better you write. Kids are sometimes surprised when they find writing is a fun way to express your thoughts.

When Janine teaches creative writing workshops with school children, she teaches writing as a constructive way to express emotion. Putting words on paper, and sometimes even ripping the paper up, can be an outlet for anger.

Teaching children to love reading and preventing failure must involve parents. Many parents want to help but don't know how. Good teachers can often get a parent's help in encouraging reading at home.

During his years as principal, Bob's school developed a written retention policy to try to make sure that the school and parents worked together to help failing children succeed: Any teacher who suspected that a child might fail was to alert the principal and parents no later than mid-term, and schedule a conference to discuss their concerns. Together they would develop a plan to help the child. Parents were expected to play a large role in this plan. The reading specialist would diagnose the problems and be assigned to work with the child if necessary. Parents and teacher were encouraged to continually review the child's progress and make necessary changes. In March, the teacher would report on the child's progress. If retention was still a possibility, a conference with the parents, teacher and principal would be scheduled and together needed changes would again be made. In June, if the child was still being considered for retention, parents, teacher and principal would meet to make the final decision. Retention then was still only considered if the group felt it would be best for the child.

Bob knew that students who fail a grade are often the ones labeled as troublemakers. A principal, he spent much of his time with these students. The problems, in those early years, were usually not serious. Some of these children caused trouble to cover their learning problems. Others tried in school but they had a learning or cognitive disability that held up their learning.

Many of the kids who were sent to the office repeatedly had a well-developed sense of humor. And for the most part, these kids had friends. Many of them were good at sports and were leaders on the playground.

Ralph was such a boy. Janine remembered him in fourth grade when she was a student. He was a funny kid, always clowning around. When her class played dodge ball on the playground, he was the kid who took the lead, racing up and down the line to grab balls and throw them. He was part of a group of boys who liked to tease girls – giving them silly nicknames and making them laugh when they were supposed to be doing math problems at the board. When the teacher gave a little time at the end of the day to work on homework, Ralph would often volunteer to wash the blackboards or go clean the erasers; he just couldn't sit still.

When fifth grade came, Ralph was missing—he had failed and was still in fourth grade. "How can that be?" Janine thought. "He must be eleven years old, the same as me. How can they make him act like a ten-year-old?"

Several weeks later, Ralph came into their fifth grade classroom to deliver a note. As he entered, the boys who used to be his friends sneered, no words, just a sarcastic muttering of his last name. Janine was startled to see his reaction. The boy who once had a funny comeback for everything just hung his head, handed the note to the teacher, and left again without a backwards glance.

Most of the teachers at Bob's school understood his retention policy and went along with it, but there was one big exception—Norma, a fourth grade teacher. Norma really resented the mischievous kids, the ones who struggled to read and joked around to make up for it. Norma was the most difficult teacher Bob had ever met. His predecessor, who had inherited her when he came to the job, complained about Norma and said, "She's your problem now, Bob."

Norma was an angry person. She would incite confrontation at every turn: the schedules were not right, the neighboring classrooms were too loud, the principal was too lenient on her kids, she didn't have time to help troubled children.

Bob overlooked Norma's rudeness to him and even to the rest of the staff, but he couldn't forgive her for what she did to some of her students.

Every year a handful of boys (always boys) in Norma's class were labeled troublemakers – and she used the word without any affection or warmth. These boys were sent to the office again and again. The reasons were things like failing to do homework, talking and laughing in class (she classed this as insolent and insubordinate), and bothering other students. A typical note might read: "I'm fed up with his behavior—he just doesn't want to pay attention. He doesn't care about school and he bothers other kids so they can't learn. My other children are starting to copy his behavior. Please give him a good talking to and a stern warning that if his behavior doesn't improve, he will fail third grade."

Bob will never forget the June day when she arrived, unexpectedly at the office door with four mothers in tow. "Bob," she said without preamble, "I have had conferences with these parents. They agreed that their children need to be kept back in third grade another year." She handed Bob a slip of paper with the names of the children, all boys.

Bob stared at her in disbelief, caught totally off guard. He couldn't believe she would bring four mothers to the office to discuss such a personal, difficult, and embarrassing issue. The school policy was written to protect a family's privacy and to help children in trouble succeed. Norma knew the school policy. Yet, Norma never had any conferences or mentioned anything about the kids in her class failing. She knew the policy but she didn't agree with it.

"Norma, I don't remember seeing any retention slips in January. Why wasn't this brought up then?"

"I knew at mid-year that these boys were having trouble and I have tried all different methods to help them learn," She looked at Bob defensively. "I thought that all the good things I would try would be useless if the kids thought they were going to fail."

Bob could feel his anger rising as he stared at the four mothers. He knew that Norma had been using retention as a threat to the boys all year. It was their behavior more often than their lack of academic progress that made her promise them over and over, "You are going to fail third grade." She had used the threat so often that she felt obligated now to stick to it.

"Well," Norma broke into his thoughts. "It doesn't matter. The point is that none of these boys are ready for 4th grade. They can't possibly succeed next year." She looked at the parents, and then flashed Bob a triumphant look.

How could a teacher report with such glee that four of her students had learned nothing all year? How was it that she regarded failing as such a positive triumph? By her own admission, she knew at midterm that they were failing, and she tried all different methods, yet they all failed. She couldn't possibly think that the boys would learn from staying with her another year.

But Norma wasn't really thinking about the boys. That was the problem. She felt that she was a good teacher because she was a tough teacher--a tough teacher who brooked no nonsense and failed borderline kids. It wasn't part of her job to worry about how these boys would feel next year when their friends would be a grade ahead of them; when their new classmates would label them dummies; when they would get taunted because they didn't fit in with either group. Bob knew the four kids – Bobby, Eric, Jay, and Tom. They had been in the office numerous times over the years.

Bob had been concerned with Tom. He was filled with anger, with no friends. Other children disliked him. He often tattled on his classmates for even small infractions. They would call him names and he would retaliate by yelling at them. His yelling in class often earned him a trip to the office. He wasn't a good student but he did try. His home life was certainly a factor.

Bob vividly remembers the time he brought a note from Norma, who was upset that he was the only child that had not brought his 35 cents for the weekly reader.

He was from a poor family, but 35 cents wasn't that much money.

"Tom," Bob asked, "Could you ask your mom for the money tonight?"

"My mommy won't be home tonight. She's working."

"Then could you ask your dad?"

He looked at Bob thoughtfully, and then asked, "My day daddy or my night daddy?"

Bob reached into his pocket, pulled out a dime and quarter, and handed him the money.

It was clear, from looking into the faces of the parents, that Norma had convinced these mothers that retaining the boys were the only answer to the problem. Bob took a deep breath and began talking to them. He explained that there were reading groups in every classroom. That meant that their children would be reading at their own level throughout school. Each child would learn reading at his present level whether he was in fourth grade or third. He promised to monitor the children, keep the parents informed of their progress, and have the reading specialist help.

At this point, Norma interrupted. She thought that what Bob was saying was a lot of nonsense. She felt that it was her job to administer to a child's intellectual needs and abilities, not worry about how he felt because he failed a grade.

"If these boys stay in third grade for one more year, I can have them reading at grade level by the end of the year," Norma insisted, "Then they will be caught up with the rest of the grade and will read at grade level for the rest of their time in school."

She knew, of course, that the four children would be placed with a different teacher. If the children didn't have to pay the horrible price of repeating the grade with Norma, Bob would have loved to place the four children in her class again next year. The look on her face when she saw their names on her class list would have been priceless. She hated these kids.

Bob said, "I know from experience that children who fail rarely ever achieve grade level in reading. Retention slows their progress in all subjects."

"Well, I simply don't believe in passing children along. These boys were warned that they would be retained and they deserve to remain in third grade." Norma's voice was curt, and Bob knew they'd better stop before they ended up battling in front of the parents.

What was most maddening was the way Norma had turned this into a battle that had nothing to do with the best interests of the children. She had decided that she was going to fail those four boys, and her pride would not allow her to give in. Bob kept trying to shift the discussion to talk about the boys, to make it clear that we were all on the same side--we all wanted what was best for them. But Norma was too defensive, guarding what she considered her high standards as a teacher.

Bob told the parents he would abide by their decision. "You know how I feel about retention-- that it will hurt rather than help your children. I have given the matter a great deal of thought, and I want what is best for your child. I feel strongly that your boys should go on to fourth grade. Now you know how I feel, so I must ask: Do you really want your children failed?"

The women looked at each other and then at Norma.

Mrs. Davis spoke up first: "Yes." The other three women nodded in agreement.

Jay's mom raised her hand shyly, like a small child in class, and waited to be given permission to talk. Her face was turning red, and Bob knew exactly what she was about to say.

"Mr. Kinsella, I was kept back in third grade and it -- it was the best thing that ever happened to me." The other women turned and looked at her as she spoke. She flushed an even deeper shade of red. "I was sick and missed a lot--that's why," she blurted out, "I had to catch up." Embarrassed, she retreated into silence and spent the next few minutes studying the nameplate on my desk.

All those years had gone by and yet this woman still felt as deeply as ever about the humiliation of failing. And what was most incomprehensible, she wanted to put her son through the same shame.

"This is a very serious decision. It will affect your child for the rest of his life. Please, go home and discuss it with your husbands. Then give me your decision in writing tomorrow."

The mothers rose and began, quietly, to leave. Norma's shrill voice broke the stillness: "Well, I know these children will be better off if they are retained. I've had them all year, and I know them."

The next day, all the parents sent notes to the office. Tom, Bobby, and Jay were to fail. Eric's mother wrote that her husband wanted his son to pass. When Norma heard the news, she was angry that Eric's parents hadn't gone along with her recommendation.

"I know that child. Eric is the one who needs retention most. His parents will be sorry."

Bob was angry: "Norma, you really put me on the spot the other day. You could have told me what was going on earlier, and talked to me before notifying the parents. If you had followed school policy and notified us of the problem in January -- as was our policy -- we could have had a private conference with the parents, shared our concern and developed a plan that would have helped these children."

"I am the one in the classroom with these children. I am the one who knows them."

"Norma we are going to follow the progress of these children through this school and then we will know who was right."

Bob would have loved to be proved wrong. He felt that Bobby and Jay might be exceptions to the rule—they might complete school. He knew they could hold their own on the playground. They were big and they were good athletes. Everyone would still want them on their team. Perhaps their athletic successes would be enough to keep them in school.

Bob hoped that Bobby's and Jay's desire to be on the varsity wrestling team would keep them in school. He knew that Tom, the loner, would slip further into his shell. When he turned 16, he would quit school. To be honest, Tom would have quit whether he was passed or failed. He just had too many problems—at school and at home.

The next year, Bob and Norma reviewed the results of the Iowa test scores for the four boys. The review showed that none of the boys were reading at grade level. Tom scored even lower on the test than he did the year before. Jay and Bobby showed 3 to 4 months progress in most areas. Eric, the boy who went on to 5th grade, the boy Norma declared the worst of them all, had gained 8 to 9 months in all academic areas. He hadn't gained a full year, and still wasn't at grade level but he did make significant progress.

Norma stared stonily at the results. When we completed the review of the test, she stood up. "I know those three boys are better off for being retained. I don't believe in standardized tests." Yearly, we reviewed the Iowa test results and despite the convincing test evidence that showed the boys making little progress, she was still convinced that she had done the right thing for those kids.

Bob followed the progress of the four boys, and sadly their schoolwork continued to get worse. They were failing and they knew it. Their parents and teacher had told them they were failures and their classmates' looks, as their bluebirds reading group (the dummy group as they called it) convinced them. They knew they were reading below grade level and so did the other children. Teachers like Norma would even taunt children like them with comments such as, "Even a first grader could read this? How can you not know this word? It's a first grader's word. You could learn this baby stuff if you would only try."

A basic tenet of learning is, "Every child needs attention. If they can't get attention in a positive way they will get attention in a negative way." This theory proved itself with the three boys that Norma failed. They antagonized teachers. Their trips to the office became more frequent. Parent conferences were common. Bob couldn't help but think that the parents thought that he was punishing them for failing their child against his advice. It was sad to see these three boys his office so often. Their sullen faces clearly showed they hated school.

The boys left the elementary school after fifth grade. Bobby and Jay became top wrestlers in their weight class in $7^{th}$, $8^{th}$, and $9^{th}$ grade. They both turned 16 in $9^{th}$ grade. They quit school right after the wrestling season ended. Their dreams of wrestling on the varsity team never happened.

Concerned with what he saw, Bob decided to do a study on students in the district who failed a grade. Records the school kept made it almost impossible to know if a child failed. Even without this vital information, he decided to do a simple study that lacked the rigors of sound research. He obtained a list of the names and birth dates of all the graduating seniors, a class of about 450 students. Student ages were used to determine if the senior failed a grade. It was assumed that a 19-year-old had failed once, a 20-year-old had failed twice. Clearly this was not a tight research study but it would give some idea of the success or failure of retention.

The results were surprising. Not one 20-year-old graduated, and only two 19-year-olds did. Bob knew that all four elementary schools in the district had held many children back every year. Convinced that what he was seeing was a fluke, Bob looked at the previous graduating class. The results were identical.

It appeared from this simple study that these students who failed a year in elementary school either moved to another school, or they dropped out of school. Bob concluded that children who are held back in elementary school are at a high risk of not graduating. Retention may make a parent or teacher feel better at the time, but if our goal is helping children get an education and graduate—we failed.

## Chapter 11
## Learning to Teach

The first day of school can be both exciting and nerve-wracking for new teachers. Bob can remember having special sympathy for a new kindergarten teacher whose first minutes as a teacher involved a screaming child who acted terrified to be in school. Concerned, he stopped after school to see how things went, to see if she needed help. She was busy putting some toys into a big wooden chest in the front of the room.

She looked up when Bob asked if she needed anything. She smiled, rolled her eyes, and said, "I almost did this morning. Do you know Brian? He just kept screaming. I tried to hold him on my lap, but that didn't help."

"What did you do?"

"Nothing." She flashed a broad smile and waved her hands in the air. "That's just it! When he recognized another kid who came in, he walked over, helped himself to some blocks, and began playing. He's been fine ever since."

Margy, a new third-grade teacher, was very shy around Bob. Whenever he visited her classroom, she acted nervous and flustered, but he had the sense that the children really liked her. One morning he listened outside her door as she read a story to the children. They were all cluttered around her listening to her every word. Alone with the kids, she was full of confidence and enthusiasm. She was reading a story, using sweeping hand gestures and funny accents, to keep the children involved. The children loved it. As Bob, quietly entered her room, she turned towards the door where he was standing to wave at an imaginary person, her eyes still on the book, and boomed, "Hello Meatball!" The children all giggled. They had seen the principal enter. She looked up and saw the principal. Her face flushed: "I didn't mean you!"

After a few observations, Bob could see that Margy was a good teacher. Every morning she greeted the children by name. They quietly talked to each other until the bell rang, then quickly took their seats. She didn't waste time taking attendance. She already knew who was absent by glancing at the desks. Daily she briefly explained what they were going to do that day. Assignments were already written on the board. During breaks, Margy was often chatting with other teachers, getting new ideas.

Many new teachers see the humor in children. They are able to laugh with them. They quickly seek help for a troubled child. The cute stories they share about children shows they enjoy them and see the good in every child.

Good teachers will often get involved in the things that are important to a child. Bob remembers the time a kindergarten teacher asked him to help her out when little Kathy left a present on the bus.

Kathy, who was normally all dimples and chatter, was sobbing into her hands, weeping as though her heart was breaking. The teacher figured out what bus Kathy rode, and Bob called the bus garage. The bus driver searched the bus, found the bag, and said she would bring it over to the school. When Bob went down to the classroom to report the news, the teacher sighed with relief. Kathy stopped crying, and actually gave Bob a smile.

Curious about the important present, Bob asked the little girl, "Can you tell me what the present is? I'll keep it a secret."

"Cross-your-heart-and-hope-to-die?"

Bob repeated the childish vow as solemnly as he could and knelt down so she could whisper the secret into his ear. Kathy looked to make sure her beloved teacher could not hear and leaned to whisper: "A bag of pretzels."

A school is as good as its teachers. Selecting the best is a difficult, time-consuming part of a principal's job. Reviewing transcripts and reading recommendations was the first step in the process, but it was the interview that told Bob the most about each candidate. Bob tried to interview all candidates that showed promise. He used the interview to give prospective teachers the opportunity to share their views on teaching and their goals and ambitions in a relaxed atmosphere and to ask questions about the school and the new position. Bob asked many questions including how they would handle

*Learning to Teach*

common teaching problems. The interview gave him insights into how the teacher would function in the classroom and fit as a member of our staff.

In fact, it was during an interview that the two authors of this book met. Bob was interviewing for an elementary computer teacher. Janine applied. Because she was local, he knew she was the valedictorian of her high school class but he also knew that her degree was in English Literature. He was looking for a person with a math background. Out of courtesy, he set up an interview with her. Her recommendations were wonderful but her transcript confused him. She had taken many advanced college math courses and had received an A in each class. During the interview he was impressed with her answers, and her pointed questions made him realize she was an excellent candidate but he needed a teacher with a strong math background. He asked her why an English major would take so many math courses. She looked a little embarrassed and then admitted, "I took Calculus just to get an easy A."

She was hired and Bob and Janine became close friends. Bob began talking to Janine about the book he had been planning for years to write, a book filled with stories about the many students he had gotten to know over his years as a principal. Janine was especially interested because she had been a student in that same school district during that time period. She remembered all kinds of details and anecdotes from her school years, details that enriched his stories. Her own strong opinions about education led to many spirited discussions with Bob, and before they knew it, they were writing a book together.

Bob made a habit of spending time with the new teachers he hired because he well knew that the first year of teaching is difficult. Many new teachers spend too much time worrying whether or not the children like them. Other teachers are too standoffish, emulating favorite college professors. Professors dispense knowledge, but leave the responsibility of learning to the students. This method works with college students who are paying tuition to learn a subject but it doesn't work well with a roomful of lively second graders. These problems can usually be quickly overcome with tactful suggestion, and with the help of other teachers and the support staff.

Some people don't learn though. One time, for example, Bob was concerned about a new fifth grade teacher named Jane. One morning as he was walking by her room, he heard children shouting:

"That's done!"
"Do I have to do this?"
"I'll get you!"

Then he heard the racing of feet and the teacher yelling, "Don't hit him!"

Bob rushed into the room. It was bedlam. Students were wandering around aimlessly. One boy was chasing another with the wooden pointer; a girl was yelling at the top of her voice to another girl to come back to her desk; and two boys were fighting over a book in the back corner. Kids in the back of the room were banging the closet doors, making such a racket that Bob knew it must be disturbing other classes.

Things quieted down once the kids noticed the principal was in the room. He waited until the kids were in their seats, then quietly left. Back in the office, he turned to Alice and said, "Schedule a formal observation with Jane tomorrow morning."

The next morning as he neared her room for the observation, he heard her screaming: "Remember, don't any of you fool around while Mr. Kinsella is visiting."

"If you act up, I promise you will regret it."

Then in an almost menacing voice she added, "Understand?"

Bob knew that screams and threats are a teacher's last effort to get control of a class. Unable to challenge children with innovative projects and ideas, they resort to fear tactics. They try to frighten them with loud voices and outlandish punishments. They correct children's behavior with sarcasm. They belittle the children in front of their peers.

During the observation Johnny yelled out, "I'm not playing with Joe. He cheats."

Jane went over to the group, and Bob heard her say to Johnny in a sarcastic tone, "If the baby can't win, he won't play." Bob knew that sarcasm may keep them quiet, but it certainly doesn't help them learn. No child should have to put up with this teaching style. It is the meanest kind of teaching.

By the end of the year, Bob knew that Jane was not going to make it as a teacher in his school. He tried every way he could to help her, even assigning another teacher to work with her and giving her all kinds of specific ways to handle the children in the classroom. He stopped by her room frequently and had many conversations with her. But Jane ignored the help of the principal and the mentor she had been assigned, choosing instead to seek the help of Norma, the teacher who used sarcasm as a method of discipline.

It did not surprise Bob in the least when some of the children in Jane's class showed up in his office at the end of the year saying that they wanted to have a surprise party for their teacher. He had seen this pattern before. The children had been behaving badly all year and felt guilty. They were basically nice kids, and they wanted to have a party for her as a way of saying they were sorry. Bob told them that the party was against school rules and sent them back to the classroom.

Often, Bob could see clues that let him know when he needed to observe a teacher. When teachers frequently send children to the office for minor offenses like failure to complete a homework assignment, sharpening a pencil without permission, talking without raising their hand, or bothering other children – that meant that the teacher could not handle minor problems in the classroom and needed help. It especially bothered Bob when a note asked him to threaten the child with failure if they didn't shape up. These same teachers constantly complain about what a terrible class they have. They feel most of their students aren't ready for the grade. They talk tough, presenting the image of the no-nonsense teacher who doesn't put up with children who can't do the work they assign. Often these teachers talk about the student's parents. They say things like, "Well, if the parents can't control the kids, how am I expected to make them behave?" All of these behaviors serve as warning signs for a principal. Another important clue is when many parents request to have their child placed in another class.

Bob made a point of observing all teachers, especially the great ones. Many principals think observations are a waste of time or use them merely for evaluation of untenured teachers. Bob felt that all teachers deserve feedback and recognition, but more important, great teachers teach principals the nuances of good teaching.

For example, Bob watched Barb, a fourth grade teacher, introduce poetry to her class, a roomful of nine-year-olds who were convinced that they hated poetry. Instead of just reading and listening to poetry, she made them write their own. When a child couldn't come up with a topic for a poem, she encouraged them to write about their favorite topic. Baseball became the theme for many poems. One student told Bob years later that he still has that poem and still enjoys poetry.

That teacher used the enthusiasm of students to teach other kids who weren't getting it. Donald was one of these students that needed help. He was the school troublemaker. He had been held behind a year, and students often said, "He is bigger and meaner than everyone else." But when the teacher encouraged Donald to show his lines of poetry to other students, they responded sincerely by saying how much they liked it. Their positive comments sent him back to his seat to write more.

A fourth grade teacher invited Bob to visit his class because he was excited about a project another teacher had told him about. As Bob entered the classroom, he saw piles of books all around the room and students decorating cardboard boxes. The fourth grade teacher looked up, smiling, "This was Dorothy's idea! She does it with her kindergarten kids, but I thought it would work with fourth graders – and I think it does."

Dorothy, a kindergarten teacher, had told him about how she got children involved in reading. She had asked parents to donate children's books -- any type -- for a project. Parents would respond by sending in all kinds of books. Then the kids decorated cardboard boxes that would hold the handful of books each child would choose to bring home. It was great to see the fourth grade teacher's excitement as the kids in his class were rummaging through the books, making their choices.

John was a teacher who read aloud to his students every day during a quiet time after lunch. All students looked forward to this part of the day. He was a great reader, using voices and building suspense into his words. His enthusiasm encouraged student to want to read. When he read *The Hobbit,* one student was so excited he took the next three books out the library. These books were daunting to 5th graders (all 1500 pages of them), but before long other students followed suit.

Observing teachers in actual classroom situations is an important tool used in the evaluation of staff but casual observations and conversation with teachers, parents and students often gives clues that help a principal better understand a teacher.

One parent told Bob that her little boy just loved Mrs. Crabtree, a second grade teacher. He came home often with stories about things Mrs. Crabtree had said. Just before Easter he came home and told his mom that Mrs. Crabtree told the class a secret: "She's going on a diet so she can lose enough weight to wear her new Easter outfit."

Her son went to school early the first day after the Easter break to see the new Mrs. Crabtree. Somehow, he expected that the bulky figure of his beloved teacher would have transformed into a svelte model. Somehow, he had gotten the idea that wearing that new Easter outfit was really important to her. After school he dragged himself home, close to tears and told his mom: "I feel so sorry for Mrs. Crabtree, she is as fat as before."

That same student several years later surprised Mrs. Crabtree by visiting her after school. She greeted him warmly. Before he left she went to her big cupboard, rummaged through it and came out with a beautiful shiny rock: "Remember when you gave me this?"

It's easy to recognize great teachers. They have a keen sense of humor. They seek and share teaching strategies. They do send children to the office but the note might read something like this: "Tommy is having a bad day, he needs some time to himself to calm down." They love their class and find ways to laugh with them. They brag about their students and always have cute stories about the children. Parents are frequent visitors and the teacher makes them feel welcome. Parents will often request that their children be put into their classes. Sometimes this causes the principal problems. A principal can't put 35 children in their class and 10 in another class.

One of these teachers, Dorothy Ford, invited Bob to visit her class. The children were sitting in a circle. Each child was taking turns telling the class about a hobby he or she was interested. Bob smiled. They looked so little and precious as they told their story. When the last little red-faced boy finished talking about his stamp collection, the teacher turned to Bob. The heads followed her stare to where he sat. "Mr. Kinsella," she said, "would you like to share something with the class? Maybe something about your newest addition?"

Dorothy, of course, knew about the latest addition to Bob's family, his son Joe. "My wife had a baby boy," he told the class. "He's just one month old today. We named him Joseph."

Most of the children smiled at the news, but one little girl stood up solemnly. "Mr. Kinsella," she said reproachfully, "that's not a hobby."

## Chapter 12
## Measuring Kids

Both teachers and children dread the week of standardized tests. One time, a second grade teacher, to ease the fears of her children about testing, tried to be very positive about the tests. She told them that the tests were just like a game. Some of the children were even smiling as they opened their booklets. After a half hour of silence, with kids scribbling on scrap paper in a frustrated way or scowling as they erased answers, one boy looked up and glared at his teacher, "Don't like this game. Ain't no fun."

Standardized tests have been a part of education since the early 1900's. Their use has been praised for its contributions to education and condemned for its shortcomings. In the early 70's major battles about the effectiveness of standardized tests broiled over into the media.

Critics claimed that national tests were not a valid measure for local schools. The test included material that was taught in all states across the country and even included items taught in higher grades. Critics felt that it was unfair to expect a child to be tested and graded on material not in the local curriculum. They were concerned that the test determines the curriculum, not the local school district, and that what is taught in California may not be relevant for student in New York.

## Measuring Kids

Proponents of standardized tests argued that years of study go into the construction of the tests and its content reflected the many curriculum guides used in schools today. It was not expected that children would get 100% on the test. The tests were designed to spread scores across the normal curve of learning so schools could compare the achievement of their students with students across the country. Even the proponents of testing knew that the value of standardized tests were limited. They knew that the test was an important tool in measuring a school's progress but could not be the sole criteria for determining life-altering decisions about students.

Test scores alone do not give the full picture of what a student is learning. Think of what would happen if a basketball coach selected players based simply on how a player performed on the basics of basketball, such as foul shooting, and never even watched the players play a game. Shaq would be spending his nights practicing fouls shots instead of playing.

Every school district has to worry about PR. The community's perception of the school district even affects housing values. Unfortunately, test scores often become a way to judge a school instead of a way to help individual students.

A major push to raise scores on standardized test started in Bob's district in the 70's. This was the year the Iowa testing was changed from the fall to the spring. The change seemed logical: spring testing allowed the teacher to check on the progress students made during the year so as to make positive changes for the following year. Board Members, administrators, and parents liked the idea of testing holding teachers accountable for a child's progress. The theory was that if at teachers knew they were going to be watched for results, student achievement would rise. Unfortunately over the next few years, the test scores for Bob's school were still well above the National average but fell from the second highest scoring school in the district to next to last.

Enrollment dropped and Bob had to give up a teacher. The superintendent wanted one of his best teachers transferred to another school in the district. Not wanting to lose the teacher, Bob told him that the test scores for her students were lower than the other teacher at that grade level. The superintendent looked at Bob and said, "She's probably one of the honest ones."

Bob remembers that year well. At the first faculty meeting of the year, he knew he had to discus the results of the Iowa test with teachers. He knew that faculty meeting would be difficult. Most teachers, concerned that the test was being used to measure the effectiveness of their teaching, would be defensive.

The day of the meeting passed quietly. As Bob passed by the open classrooms, he felt reassured by how quickly the staff had fallen back into the routine. An art teacher was piling boxes of construction paper onto her cart. Another teacher was writing furiously at her desk, planning tomorrow's lesson. Two teachers chatting were catching up on gossip as they returned from the mailboxes.

Dorothy, a respected, long-time kindergarten teacher, waved Bob into her classroom and shared a story: "Peter had permission to walk home for lunch. When I let him leave, he announced to the whole class where he was going." She brushed back a wisp of her hair and smiled, "All of a sudden about ten other little ones remembered that their Mummy had told them to walk home for lunch. Of course the others were bus students. Robbie lives ten miles from here, and there he was, his hand in the air, pleading with me to let him walk home!"

They both laughed. Then Dorothy's voice changed. In a serious, concerned tone added, "The staff is really upset about all this testing nonsense. Tonight's meeting is going to be difficult."

Bob nodded. "Yes, Dorothy, I know."

She continued, "Bob, teachers know that they are accountable for a child's progress. They don't need a test to tell them."

She shrugged, and switched subjects abruptly, "Bob, I think I'm going to have a class of artists this year. Wait until you see their work."

The first faculty meeting of the year is usually more like a get together party that gives everyone a chance to talk and get re-acquainted. But Bob knew this meeting would be different.

Dorothy's warning was right on target. Through the grapevine, the teachers already knew our school had the dropped from second to fourth on Iowa scores for the five elementary schools.

Every year, like most schools across the nation, Bob's district administered the Iowa tests to their first through ninth graders. Iowa tests had been used in our school for years. In fact the test booklets were worn looking since the same test booklets were used every year. They were kept under lock and key in the district office during the year and sent to schools the day of testing.

The teachers were in the cafeteria waiting for the meeting. They were seated by grade levels and in front of each teacher was a pile of test scores. The room was silent. It usually took Bob a few minutes to quiet the room for faculty meetings. The staff was often worse than the worst class of misbehaved children. But tonight all were quiet, leaving an eerie tension in the room.

Bob briefly explained that the school's scores were still well above the national average, but were below the other schools in our district. The superintendent had pointed this out during the administrative workshop. The superintendent felt that the school was not putting enough emphasis on the basics, and he wanted each grade level in the school to review the weaknesses shown on the Iowas and select one area to focus on in their lesson plans this year.

Sam, a fourth grade teacher respected by his peers, spoke up: "Bob, if our scores are above the national average we should be congratulated instead of made to feel like failures."

Mae, a long time first grade teacher, shook her head. "Bob, our children score well. They love school and they learn to enjoy reading and thinking critically about what they read. Those of us who have been in this business a while know that raising these test scores mostly involves memorization. All we will be doing is assigning ditto sheets, correcting them and assigning more. That's not teaching."

A teacher that had been in our district for years said, "These test scores from the other schools in our district – they don't look right to me. Like this one -- it seems strange that a school that has children with major learning problems and most of its students receiving special help – that school is scoring higher than the top schools in the nation?"

Bob just shrugged his shoulders.

Another teacher angrily said, "The Iowa tests that used to be locked up in Central Office until the day of the testing were sent to each school for storage a few years ago. Did you also know that some principals have now sent the test to teachers' rooms for storage?"

Bob understood the implications of what the teachers were saying. He said simply, "If that kind of thing is happening, I am opposed to it."

Sam jumped in: "I think all teachers should have the tests in their room so they can read and study them."

The room went quiet as every head turned to look at Sam.

One teacher said, "Sam, that's cheating!"

Everyone in the room respected Sam enough to listen while he continued, "The test is designed to measure what we teach. Shouldn't we know what the test measures so that we can prepare our students?"

Suddenly, everyone started talking at once.

"I won't cheat to raise my children's scores."

"I can't believe you are saying that, Sam. It's wrong."

Sam stood up, faced the faculty, and said quietly, "Let me finish!"

"As we all know the Iowa test has many editions. I believe that each teacher should be given a copy of the edition of the test that was used the previous year."

He added, "Then in the spring a new edition of the test will be given. Knowing how and what the test measures, yet not knowing the exact questions, our students' test scores should raise."

A teacher said, "Sam, that's a great idea, but it will never fly."

Another said, "This would eliminate the temptation for teachers to teach for the test and help relieve the perception that teachers cheat to raise scores so they look good."

"It's not just a perception," said another teacher, an oldtimer, "Whenever schools get pressure to raise test scores, there will be temptation for teachers to cheat."

Sam continued, "A test measures what we teach. If we want to know if the children understand what we taught, we must test them. So in essence we all teach for the test. It's only cheating when we give the students the exact items on the tests instead of teaching the concepts."

They all liked Sam's idea but they knew that wasn't the answer for this year.

"It will never happen," said one of our longtime teachers. "Buying a new test each year is expensive. Our district will never spend that kind of money."

Bob let them talk it out and then got back to what the superintendent had directed. They were to select an area of the Iowa test to focus on this year.

They selected Language Arts and one teacher from each grade level agreed to work with Bob to research this area of the test for ideas on how to raise our scores. They discovered that if our children could get three or four more questions correct, they would score in the top 10% of the nation. They looked for something to focus on, but most of the skills on the test were ones already in our curriculum. Then they discovered that a focus on letter writing could raise our scores. Letter writing wasn't something we had previously emphasized in the lower grades, but it was something that would be a positive addition to the curriculum.

The staff embraced the idea because they saw letter writing as a useful skill. Quickly, they came up with ideas: Children could write to grandparents. They could write thank you notes. They could have penpals. One teacher found a place where kids could write to get free stuff. The teachers were relieved that we were not recommending handing out ditto sheets with Iowa-type questions. This was a change they all could make--and one that was comfortable and had the potential to excite their kids.

At the next faculty meeting Bob was glad to see the teachers again acting like a class of misbehaved children, chatting and joking before the meeting started. In fact, everyone was laughing as he walked in, and when he asked what was funny, Kathy, the speech teacher, repeated her story. That morning she had been teaching the sound "th" to a group of her first grade students and they just weren't getting it. To help them she said to one boy, "I'm not fat, I'm th-----." The boy looked at her and said, "I think you're fat."

The staff roared. And Bob knew that things were back to normal. The teachers talked about all the ways in which they were incorporating letter writing into the classroom. They offered ideas, suggestions, and recommendations about the testing program. Bob sent many of their comments to Central Office for their review.

Bob was still concerned about the pressure testing was putting on the children. He knew that parents often are too quick to accept the labels that a standardized test puts on their child. Testing can be effectively used to alert parents and teachers to problem areas, to ways in which the child needs help, but when testing places negative labels on children, labels that they will carry like flags for the rest of their lives, the whole culture of testing needs to be examined and re-evaluated.

A representative of the National Congress of Parents and Teachers gave this comment in support of the continuation of standardized tests, "It simply won't do to throw all these tests away. Parents must have some means of knowing whether their children can read." Many wondered if that representative ever read to her children or let them read to her.

Letter writing became an important part of the language arts curriculum. Teachers realized how successful it was long before the children took the test in the spring. Parents' comments revealed how successful it was:

"This year my children sent thank-you notes to everyone who gave them a Christmas present."

"Imagine getting a thank-you note for a thank-you note."

"Grandma was thrilled to get a letter from my kids. She loved reading about what they were doing."

"Grandma wrote to the children telling them how much they loved the letter and then told them about her life when they were their age".

"My kids learned things about my mom and dad that I didn't even know. I didn't know my mom played on a championship basketball team."

Another parent completed the picture of the success of the program. With tears in her eyes told Bob, "My mom wrote me a letter after receiving letters from my two children that I will always treasure. Mom said, 'You should be proud of your children. They are kind, caring and loving children, just like their mom. I'm so proud of you.'"

The media and public perception of schools continues to make testing a hot issue, with schools getting ranked solely by the tests. Teachers know that testing can be an important tool in assessing a student's progress, but they also know it is only one factor amongst many.

A school must be a warm place where children feel safe and loved. It must be a place where children are excited about learning, a place where children develop a love of reading instead of just reading to answer test questions. Teachers must challenge children and give them outlets for their energy and creativity. Children who are excited about learning will be motivated to continue their education.

There are things a standardized test cannot measure. Seven years after performing in an elementary school play, students knew the words, remembered the excitement, and treasured the friendships they had formed.

Many adults still remember the enthusiasm of that teacher who made reading and writing an important part of their lives, who first taught them to put their feelings into words.

Parents can tell their child is excited about learning when the child starts talking excitedly about his favorite book, or begs to be taken to the library, or asks for vinegar and baking soda to replicate a science experiment.

And the words of a child are often the best way to judge whether or not a teacher had made her classroom a warm, safe place for her students. "She wouldn't do that! She loves me."

## Chapter 13
## Hearts, Flowers and Melted Ice Cream

Valentine's Day was different than any school holiday. The children were always in a good mood, not hyper, and the teachers could still get them to work. Janine can remember the excitement in her household when she was a kid on the morning of Valentine's Day. She and her sisters would be looking for their favorite pink or red clothes, and her mother would tie red ribbons onto her braids. Few of the boys dressed up for Valentine's Day, but almost all of the girls did. Even teachers dressed special for the day. One year Mary Honors, a third grade teacher, dressed in fluffy red dress. The room mother who came in for the party congratulated her.
"Why are you congratulating me?" asked Mary.
"Aren't you pregnant?"
Mary, unmarried and very certainly not pregnant, couldn't wait to tell Bob the story.
He jokingly asked, "Is it true?"
"Oh yes," said Mary, "by immaculate conception!"
She rolled her eyes. "Bob, I'll never wear that dress again."
Valentine's Day seemed to bring out the best in everyone. Children seemed kinder and more considerate of their classmates and their teachers on

this special day. Everyone talked with each other, and for this day, all members of the class were friends.

The highlight of Valentine's Day was giving and receiving cards. Kindergarten and first grade children enjoyed the colorful cartoon characters on the card but many couldn't read them. They had to wait until they got home to have their parents read the cards to them. But Valentine's Day took on a special meaning to second graders. This was the first time all could read their cards. They laughed and giggled and hugged their friends who sent them the cards.

Janine can still remember how carefully she and her girlfriends selected the cards. They felt especially self-conscious in choosing cards for the boys they felt were special. The girls never signed their names but if the boys looked hard enough, which they never did, they would have found initials or other identifying sign on the card. The girls watched each boy as they opened their cards, hoping they would recognize the sender. The boys, on the other hand, enjoyed the cards but saw nothing special. They just continually counted and recounted the cards. They were only interested in the total number they received, not a message. The card they sent to each of us girls had no meaning, except that it was the next card in the pack.

Barbara, the art teacher, helped the children make a Valentine card for their parents. Most children selected red or pink construction paper.

They folded the stiff paper in two and drew a half heart shape and cut it out. When opened, it was a full heart. A lace doily and often a lopsided heart with an arrow through it glued to the paper. The glue the children used was thick and pasty and smelled like candy. Yes, like their parents before they tried to eat it.

Inside the card the child would write a poem. Most verses started with the original phrase: "Roses are red, Violets are blue . . . ." Barbara often had to help the younger children write the words. The cards were certainly not very original-- but the parents loved them. Many parents saved the cards and years later would show Bob, and proudly say, "Can you believe he's in college?"

Children wanted to send cards to all of their classmates. Teachers sent class lists home with the children the week before so that the children could spell the names right. One year the class list caused a problem for Marge Ingalls, a third grade teacher.

After the lists were sent home, Alice received a phone call from an irate parent who wanted to speak to the principal. Alice came to my door and said to Bob: "I've got an angry parent on the phone. She wouldn't give her name but she was furious with Mrs. Ingalls."

Bob picked up the phone. "This is Mr. Kinsella, may I help you?"

"That Mrs. Ingalls shouldn't be allowed to teach children."

"What did she do?"

"I don't want to talk to you, I want to talk to her, and I want to do it now!"

"Please give me your name, and I will schedule a time for you and Mrs. Ingalls to meet."

"Mrs. Hogan!" she yelled and hung up.

Bob talked to the teacher, who had no idea what Mrs. Hogan's concern might be. He called the parent back and asked her to come in to school that day. Concerned at the level of anger, he scheduled the meeting in the room right next to his office. He made the appointment right after school because he knew that Marge needed to get home to her husband, who was dying of throat cancer.

After the last bus was called, Marge arrived and took a seat in the conference room. When Mrs. Hogan arrived, Bob showed her to the room. He could tell she was angry. She was clutching the class list in her hand, the one that had been sent home for Valentine's cards. She waved the list at Marge and yelled, "Did you write this class list?"

Bob looked at Marge, indicating that he would stay if she wanted him present. She shook her head, and he backed out of the room.

The meeting was brief. When the door opened, Mrs. Hogan walked out stonily. Marge said, loud enough for Bob to hear: "Just for your daughter, I'll make a new list and notify all parents that they should throw away the last list. Is there anything else I can do for you?"

Mrs. Hogan did not even look at her. She walked out, slamming the door.

Marge sighed.

"You're not going to believe it, Bob. You know what she was so angry about?"

"No idea."

"Can you imagine a teacher being so ignorant as to use a child's classroom name rather than her given name? I wrote Kathy Hogan on the list rather than Kathleen Hogan."

She rolled her eyes, "I just can't imagine how I could have made such a terrible mistake."

"Leave us the list," Bob said, "We'll retype it." He knew she was in a hurry to get home to her dying husband.

"Some people don't know what a real problem is."

Almost all of the children came to school with Valentines for all the names on the class list as well as the teacher, and some even gave cards to the principal. Some were beautiful, handmade cards but most were store bought. Often the most frequent visitors to the office, the school troublemakers, were the ones that could be seen sneaking into office to leave a Valentine card. One year Donny, the boy who had passed porn cards out in class, appeared in the outer office as Bob was about to leave to make a quick tour of the building. He assumed Donny was in trouble but planned to see him later.

Many cards were piled on the desk. One contained a small box with a big homemade card attached. The sender had signed it, "Guess Who!"

Inside the box was a small cake delicately shaped like a cupid. Red frosting formed a tiny bow and arrow on top of white frosting. As Bob stared at the cake, Donny peered into the office. His impish grin said he wasn't in trouble.

"Oh, you got a present," he asked, acting quite surprised. "Is it a cake shaped like Cupid?"

"Donny, did you send me this cake?"

"Not me, Mr. Kinsella." He grinned and left just as quickly as he appeared.

Alice walked into the office. "It's beautiful Bob."

Bob exclaimed, "I just can't imagine who baked it for me."

"I told him I would put it on your desk for you--but he insisted he do it himself."

One second grader ran out of cards and discovered she had forgotten the principal. She took out a sheet of regular writing paper and wrote a note saying that she had run out of cards but still wanted to wish her principal a happy Valentine's Day.

On Valentine's Day, you could usually tell who the brand new teachers were. The approach to distributing cards exemplified the difference between learning how to teach in college and actually doing it. College teachers and many textbooks recommended a big central box as a way to collect the Valentine cards. The children attractively decorated a big box with a slit on the top, which was then placed in the front of each room. The kids loved sliding their cards into the box. Later in the afternoon as they were finishing their party, the teachers would open the pretty box and then realize all the names had to be read so that each card was given to the correct child. In a class of 25 children the box would hold as many as 625 cards. Kids clamoring for their valentines would surround the teacher as she frantically distributed the cards.

Veteran teachers used the mailbox system, giving each child a simple paper lunch bag with the child's name on it, and lining the bags up on a table. The youngest children would give their cards to their teachers who put them in the mailboxes. Children old enough to read could put the cards in the right bags themselves. When it was time for the party, each child just had to take his own bag full of cards.

In the afternoon most classes had a party that usually included pink cupcakes, cookies, heart-shaped candies, and every kind of soda sent in by parents. The children read their cards and looked at each other's cards, the girls clustering in groups to giggle over them, while the boys traded cookies and had contests to see how much soda they could drink. The older children carefully counted their cards hoping they had more than their friends.

Some children gave small presents to their teachers. A mother told Bob about the present her son Brian gave his teacher. He bought it with his own money. He wrapped it himself and it wasn't until a few days later that she thought to ask, "What did you buy your teacher?"

He replied, "I bought her a bar of ivory soap, a large bar just like we use. I bet she'll really liked it."

"That's nice," his mother said. To Bob, she added, "I wonder if his teacher will think that we are trying to give her a hint--like on those TV ads for deodorant?"

When Janine was teaching sixth grade, she tried to expose her students to literature by putting famous quotes up on the bulletin board. On Valentine's Day she put up the famous line, "O My love's like a red, red rose--Robert Burns" and read the poem while the class made roses to decorate the rest of the bulletin board.

A couple of days later, just after she took down the quote, she asked the question as a bonus on a test: "Who wrote the famous line " O my love's like a red, red rose?" One boy answered: "Hallmark."

Valentine's Day was a special day for children. They received more cards on that day than they received all year. Even the card companies would take pity on parents by selling batches of cards for just pennies. This was a holiday that every child, no matter how poor the family, could participate in. The sayings on the cards were all rather trite -- but giving and getting cards from everyone would bring the class closer together -- at least for that day. Everyone would talk with each other, and for this day, all members of the class were friends.

## Chapter 14
## Flag at Half Mast

In the 1960s, few handicapped children went to a regular school. Parents were told to educate their child at home or in a special school away from the "normal" child. "Out of sight out of mind" was the philosophy of the day. It was not until 1975 that U.S. Congress passed an education law that let handicapped children go to public schools.

Jimmy DeMarco was one of the students who fought the idea that schools were no place for handicapped children. Jimmy was a six-year-old with cystic fibrosis, a fatal disease that causes the cells that line the respiratory tract to secrete thick sticky mucus that clogs the lungs, leading to one infection after another. He was also a smart, friendly boy who didn't understand why he had to stay home when all the kids in the neighborhood got to go to school. Mae Ryan, our first grade teacher, got to know Jimmy when she was tutoring him at home, and together they plotted a way to convince Bob to let him attend the elementary school.

In the fall of 1966, Jimmy arrived for his first day in a small yellow bus used for handicapped children. As he waited for that bus, Bob worried that he had made a big mistake allowing Jimmy to come to the school. Maybe Jimmy would be better off in a school where the other children were like him. Then the door of the bus opened. Out stepped a blond-haired little boy. He wore a new green shirt with a wide collar and tan corduroy pants. With great determination, he moved across the sidewalk, placing each foot carefully in front of the other. He was breathing hard, and his skinny arms seemed too small for the metal lunch box and brown paper sack he was clutching. As he approached, Bob welcomed him to school. Jimmy looked up with a big grin. His smile transformed the pale, fragile child into a happy little boy. "Thank you, Mr. Kinsella," Jimmy said shyly, "thank you for letting me come to your big school."

Jimmy lived only nine years, from 1959 to 1968. Almost from birth his mother knew that something was wrong. Jimmy could brighten her life with his smile but he was unable to move as her other children when they were his age. After a home visit, and many tests the doctor advised his parents that their son had a severe case of cystic fibrosis and that he would die before his third birthday.

Jimmy's mom changed doctors that day. They all loved their new pediatrician, Dr. Frederick Roberts. Under the guidance of Dr. Roberts, Jimmy passed his third birthday and enjoyed playing with a few friends. Jimmy carefully chose friends. He sensed those who would reject him. He could ride a bike if it was on level pavement. He loved to read, but his great love was the Chicago Cubs. He knew every player and every year he was certain his Cubs were going to win the World Series.

In the summer of 1966, Mae Ryan tutored Jimmy at home as a favor to his mother. Mae had fallen in love with the trusting little blond-haired boy. She was helping him with some math problems one day when he began asking questions:

"Mrs. Ryan, am I as good a student as the kids in your class?"

"You're better than most."

"Do you like teaching me?"

"Jimmy, you know I do." She put her arm around the frail, little body and gave him a hug. "I love teaching you."

Jimmy stared down at his paper and twirled his pencil. Mae waited patiently, wondering what was coming next. Finally, Jimmy looked up and asked quietly, "Mrs. Ryan, if I'm as good a student as your other children and you love teaching me, why can't I go to your school and be in your class?"

He jumped up excitedly and then knelt so that his eyes were level with hers. "I'll be good and work hard! Please! Please! I want to be like other kids and go to a regular school." In his eagerness, his skinny hands gripped her shoulders, but his grip was so weak she barely noticed it.

Mae knew he was right. Why should a smart child like him be kept away from school? Why shouldn't he be able to play with other kids? She was in Bob's office the next day, pleading Jimmy's case. Bob trusted Mae's judgment, and found an ally in the director of personnel, who supported the idea. Jimmy would be allowed to come to school.

Jimmy was quickly accepted by the other children in his class, especially by Skip, a popular, athletic boy. Skip adopted Jimmy the very first day of class and they were soon inseparable. Both top students, they would hurry to finish their work so that they could work together on extra projects. With a little help from Mae they explored many topics--from dinosaurs to rocks, from insects to the Civil War. Without being told, Skip always walked Jimmy to the bus, opening the heavy school door and watching from the doorway until Jimmy was safely on the bus.

Jimmy got up at 5:00 a.m. every morning to prepare for school. He spent painful hours every morning getting ready for school. His most important preparation was using a machine that sprayed a powerful decongestant mist into his lungs. This mist loosened the thick mucus that had settled in his lungs, forcing him to cough up mucus so that he could breathe. Even putting his clothes on was a tedious, excruciating process. His mother knew how hard it was for him to even move in the morning, much less dress himself. She tried to help him on his first day of school:

Jimmy, with a flicker of anger in his eyes, said, "Mom! I'm not a baby."

"Jimmy, your dad and I only want to help."

"I know, but you have to remember that I am six years old," he was determined. "If I go to regular school, I must be like other kids and get ready by myself. If it is real bad, I'll call you."

That call meant that Jimmy was unable to rid his lungs of this thick odious mucus by the inhalation of the fine mist. This meant that his parents, using a method called Posturing, would cup their hands and pound on his chest, back and sides trying to loosen the thick mucus. When it loosened they would press hard over the lungs with their fingers trying to force the mucus up so that Jimmy could breathe. It left him totally exhausted.

His mother pleaded with Dr. Roberts to find some other method to help Jimmy rid his body of this thick mucus. She loved the doctor, for he was a kind, sensitive man, but she felt that there had to be another way to help her son breathe. This sadistic procedure angered her. She often asked Dr. Roberts for another method. He would look at her, slowly shake his head, take a deep breath, and tell her to pray for a cure as he did.

After that first morning, Jimmy's parents left him alone, but they could never sleep. They would lie awake in the adjoining room listening to the choking, coughing sounds that were part of Jimmy's preparation. Only on his worst days did Jimmy miss school.

Every day in school was special to him. Jimmy's parents, knowing how important the morning routine was to him, gave him an electric alarm clock for his birthday. Jimmy had been using an old wind-up alarm clock that ticked so loudly that they were afraid it might keep him awake.

Jimmy seemed delighted with the new clock, but when his mother noticed he was using both clocks, she asked, "Don't you like the new clock?"

"Yes, it is very nice."

"Why are you still using the old clock?"

Jimmy gave her a puzzled look, "But Mom, what if the electricity went out at night? I'd miss school."

Minoa, like most schools, had those who felt that children like Jimmy didn't belong in a regular school. Respecting the wishes of the family, Bob had not told the staff what Jimmy's disease was. He wanted to be treated like everyone else. Norma, a fourth grade teacher, asked during a faculty meeting, why the little boy who coughs all the time was still in our school. She felt it was unfair for a teacher to have such a child in class. Mae curbed her anger and invited her to stay after the meeting so she could answer that question.

Mae and Norma did talk, and Mae told her what few people in the school knew. Jimmy had cystic fibrosis. She assured Norma that the disease was not contagious. What she didn't say is that in severe cases like Jimmy's, few live to see their tenth birthday. And Jimmy was nine at the time. Mae didn't like Norma and she didn't want to share Jimmy's secret.

Another problem arose when the Director of Transportation called Bob, saying that he didn't think Jimmy needed a special bus. He had decided to take Jimmy out of our school to put him on a regular bus and send him to a school that was closer.

"Walt, that is not acceptable." Bob said, "And I know Jimmy wouldn't cause his driver any trouble."

"The bus driver says that he hasn't been out to meet his bus once since this cold spell. He waits in the warm house until he sees her coming. It makes her late for her other stops. She's pretty upset. She doesn't even think he deserves special transportation. She says he looks perfectly okay to her."

"He may look okay to her but Jimmy has cystic fibrosis--he's dying. I didn't tell you before because he didn't want anyone to know."

"Oh, wow," said the supervisor, "I'll tell the driver tomorrow."

"No, don't tell her. All Jimmy wants is to be treated like other children."

Bob knew that this was unfair to the driver but he wanted to respect the family's wishes. And he smiled as he thought back to Walt's words. "She says he looks perfectly okay to her." That was a triumph of sorts for Jimmy.

The children in the school accepted Jimmy without reservation. Without being told, Skip knew Jimmy's weaknesses and took it upon himself to help. Skip walked him to the bus daily, slowing his pace to match Jimmy's tired gait. He would open the heavy school door and watch from the doorway until he was safely on the bus. Minutes later, Bob would hear Skip running back to class, jumping up to throw imaginary basketballs, slapping his hands against the tiled walls.

Jimmy was one of the reasons Bob rarely missed a day greeting the buses. Seeing the little blonde-haired boy inspired him in ways he was never able to put in words. But even on those days Bob was busy in his office, Jimmy would stop by the office lobby and peer in the window until he could see him. He'd wave and Bob would smile, looking at the little boy with his nose pressed against the glass window and step outside and say, "Hello Jimmy." And Jimmy's face would light up as if his principal was the most wonderful person in the world.

"Hello Mr. Kinsella!" he'd say. He'd give a big grin and be off down the hall, walking proudly to class.

Seeing Jimmy in the morning always got Bob's day off to a good start. He knew what Jimmy had gone through to come to school. Bob liked to believe Jimmy would always be with him. But he knew it was not true. Jimmy was dying.

One morning Jimmy showed Bob his new sneakers--PF Flyers! He pulled his pant leg above his bony ankle to show them and said, "Skip has PF Flyers too." The two boys continued down the hall,

Jimmy scuffing his feet against the tiled floor. His new sneakers were obviously several sizes too big for his tiny underdeveloped feet. Why did his parents buy him footwear that didn't fit him? Bob mentioned this to Alice and she just smiled. "They've seen that crazy sneaker commercial; all the boys have to wear them."

"But they're way too big. His parents should have gotten smaller ones."

"Oh yes. The department stores carry tiny little sneakers in the toddler section, but they're baby sneakers, not PF Flyers."

Bob could picture Jimmy in the department store convincing his mom that the sneakers fit him just right. What disappointment he must have felt when his poor stunted feet didn't come even close to filling up the smallest size. And yet, this morning, shuffling like an old man in the too-large sneakers, he was smiling and proud.

On Halloween Day Jimmy arrived with a big paper bag clutched in his hand.

"Wow, you must be hungry today," Bob teased.

Jimmy's high-pitched laugh brought a smile to his face.

"That's not a lunch bag Mr. Kinsella!" he shouted. "Look!" He unrolled the top of the bag and pulled it open. Inside there was a big tray of cookies wrapped in tin foil. He reached under the tray and pulled out his Halloween costume. It was a Chicago Cubs baseball uniform.

## Both Sides of the Desk

One day, Jimmy's teacher asked Bob to come to her classroom to talk about the trips he had taken to Crystal Canyon, a local place he often took his kids to in search of rocks. Although geology was not his specialty, Bob was confident he could answer any question a third-grader might ask about his rock collection. He held up one of the biggest rocks for the class to see and identified it as mica. "When your parents were children, they used mica for the glass in stoves and fireplaces, because mica is fire resistant and you can see through it." Smiling, he passed the rocks around for them to look at and touched. Skip seemed especially absorbed, turning a rock over in his small palm, and finally raising his hand.

"Mr. Kinsella," he said politely. "This isn't mica."

"It's not?" Every third-grader turned to stare at Skip. Jimmy, leaning over from his desk looked at the rock in Skip's hand, and nodded in agreement.

Skip held the rock up to the light and said, "It looks like mica but mica peels off in sheets, but gypsum breaks into little pieces. It's fireproof and all, but you can't get big pieces of it so you can't use it as glass for fireplaces and stoves or anything. My dad took me to Crystal Canyon. We found lots of these rocks and he told us that they were gypsum."

The students in the class looked impressed. Skip added, "Lots of people get them mixed up."

Later that night, Skip's father called. He apologized for Skip embarrassing Bob in class about those rocks. "I teach Earth Science at the university and we did study the rocks at Crystal Canyon. The rock you sent home with Skip is gypsum."

Bob laughed, "I am always learning new things from my students."

Jimmy's last day of school came on a sunny day when he was in third grade. On the playground the children were in high spirits, laughing and yelling as they raced to jump rope or play ball. Normally the sight of so much happy activity raised Bob's spirits--but not today. Today he could only focus on the fragile little boy sitting on the grass. How pale and thin he had gotten over the winter. The bright sunshine showed the blue veins under his skin and the darkness beneath his eyes. Jimmy's chest heaved as he struggled to breathe. Yet, he gathered enough strength to join in the lively discussion his friends were having.

"Make it to the play-offs? No way!" he said. "You can't make it to the World Series without a good relief pitcher."

"But their starting pitchers are terrific," Skip replied.

"Yeah, but no one's backing them up. By October the Yankees will be lucky to be in fourth place." The last remark raised the furor of several of his friends who heatedly defended their beloved Yankees. Soon, with a piece of chalk borrowed from a hopscotch game, the group of boys were mapping out the baseball season on the pavement.

The boys didn't notice their principal as they seriously considered the merits of each team. Jimmy coughed and wheezed and then turned shakily to say, "This might be the year the Chicago Cubs surprise everyone."

Minutes earlier Bob had spoken to Jimmy's mother on the telephone. Jimmy was going to the hospital right after school that day. He only had a few more days to live. And Jimmy knew. Standing by the window, waiting to see the bus come, Jimmy had looked over at his mother and said, "Mom, today will be my last day in school." She could only nod.

The bell rang: recess was over. Skip put an arm around Jimmy's shoulders to help him over the curbs as they came to get in line. As the third-grade teacher marched her class into the building, Jimmy gave one last look at the school yard, a last look at all the children waiting in crowded lines--shy girls whispering secrets in each other's ears, noisy boys tossing balls back and forth, a giggly fourth-grader trying to tell a joke, friends trading lunch boxes, a pig-tailed girl screaming that some one was pulling her hair, sweaty boys with their hair curling and their shirt tails hanging out, a group of girls clapping hands with each other as they recited some silly rhyme, a boy bent double laughing over a prank, a teacher comforting a child with a scraped knee, two boys taunting a third by stealing his baseball cap, three girls giggling over a rosy-cheeked boy in the next line.

The noise rose up from the sun-soaked pavement--the shrill cries, the laughter, the squeals, the giggles, the thumping of balls, the clapping of hands, and the stomping of impatient feet. A typical school yard scene, swarming with life and vitality. Jimmy gazed hungrily for one second longer and then he disappeared into the tan brick building.

That afternoon Bob was just finishing some paperwork when Jimmy appeared in the doorway. Jimmy's chest heaved as he struggled to breathe and said, "Mr. Kinsella, thank you for letting me come to your big school." He hesitated for a moment and then added, "This will be my last day." He looked at his principal steadily, his blue eyes shining. Bob's eyes were misting over with tears.

"Good-bye, Jimmy," he choked, "I'll never forget you."

Breathing heavily, Jimmy looked up, his blue eyes dimmed. He began walking down the hall, then slowly turned around, flashed a weak smile, winked and left the office.

The mucous in his lungs had thickened to the point that it was actually suffocating him. A few days later this courageous boy died.

Students and teachers alike were shocked at the news since so few knew how ill Jimmy had been. His disease had been kept a secret. Jimmy had been adamant that he be treated like any other kid. The school flag hung at half-staff for the rest of the week.

Bob did get an angry call from a man wanting to know why we were flying the flag at half-staff. "One of our students died this week," Bob said. When the man began to argue with him, Bob set the receiver down on the desk so that his angry words were inaudible and went out to the hallway for a drink of water. As he passed the sliding glass doors, he thought of Jimmy and how he used to peer through it to wave mornings, his nose pressed against the glass and his pale blue eyes lighting up as he smiled. He thought of the way Jimmy worked to get himself out of bed each morning and suffer through the torture that was needed to clear his lungs so he could go to his big school.

Sometime later, Mae brought Bob a manila envelope. "Here are my notes on Jimmy. For your book--the book that you'll be writing someday." She paused and then spoke with some difficulty, "You know, Jimmy's death is still difficult for me to accept--but I had to write this all down, right now while I am still hurting. He was different, Jimmy was--I'll never forget his courage and his sweetness."

Bob saved those notes, written in neat cursive writing on yellow paper:

*How do you take on another demanding task when you are very tired?*

*How do you remain calm and patiently wait for a child to obtain enough breath to go on with a lesson?*

*How do you keep two parents from the despair of knowing that their child is different?*

*How do you react when you see a good and strong man with tears of joy in his eyes at the small successes his son has achieved?*

*How do you keep from feeling smug when you have fought for this child's rights and won?*

*How do you answer the criticism of people who think you are getting too involved?*

*How do you answer an accusation that you are wasting your time and talent?*

*How do you keep from saying "I told you so" when the doubters begin to cooperate in your struggle for the best for this child?*

*How do you, as his teacher, let him go on to another teacher and not interfere?*

*How do you glory in the scene of this child having a good healthy boy fight?*

*How do you contain your amazement at his academic progress, from a struggle to learn letter sounds to research on the Civil War at eight years of age?*

*How do you keep from feeling too proud or bragging about the child's accomplishments?*

*How do you feel when a small child shows courage and determination beyond your own?*

*How do you sparkle with him at his excitement at being a scout?*

*How do you keep from questioning the justice of his affliction?*

*How do you swallow the tears when you know you won't see him coming around the corner swinging his lunch pail with a little secret wink just for you?*

*How do you keep from crying when you know the flag is flying at half-staff in honor of that child?*

You do because this child has brought love into the lives of many.

## Chapter 15
## Big Yellow Bus Ride

For kindergarten children, school started not in September, but on a morning in August when they got to ride the big yellow school bus for the first time. On the school calendar the day was listed as Kindergarten Orientation, but for the new kindergarten students it was "Big Yellow Bus Day," an exciting day for both the parents and their children. This was the day that the parents met the principal, waved to their children as they took their first school bus ride, and saw their child's classroom for the first time.

Before Kindergarten Orientation, the parents got a packet of material that included a large nametag that parents pin on their child for the first few days of school. Our kindergarten program had morning classes for children living in the village and afternoon classes for children living in the surrounding area. The big yellow busses took home the morning class and then picked up children for the afternoon class. Sometimes parents would ask for their child to be switched from one time slot to the other, but the tight schedule really didn't allow any flexibility.

One year, a parent who lived in the village insisted that Bob place her child in the afternoon class. She knew the policy but still insisted, "My child is not a morning child. I want him to go in the afternoon!"

A principal doesn't have that authority to make a busing change. That is a decision for the department of transportation. "Why don't you let him attend the morning class for a while and see how it goes?" Bob said.

The mother responded with an angry no. She added, ""I don't think any stupid rule should deprive my child of his best learning time."

She did call the department of transportation, our superintendent, and the board of education. All refused her request. They just couldn't change policy without some kind of valid reason.

A few days later the mother handed Bob a request to have her son's records sent to a private school. The "Not a Morning Child" was starting school there the next day. The boy who couldn't learn in the morning was now going to school all day. She smiled as she handed Bob the sheet that showed our district was transporting her child. She then added, "He prays for you every night. He asked if he had to stop praying now that he won't be in your school anymore"

"Let him pray for me," said Bob, "I need all the help I can get." He never saw the woman or her child again.

On the day of kindergarten orientation, mothers and children gathered in the cafeteria for the Kindergarten Orientation program. Some of the kids were bouncy and full of smiles, while others clung shyly to their mothers. Bob quickly reviewed the material each parent received in the mail, emphasizing that it was important that each child wear his nametag the first few days. This helped staff to easily recognize the kindergarteners so they could guide them to their teacher's room. Often a scared child would not even say his name aloud so the nametags were absolutely essential.

Bob kept the meeting short since he knew that parents were anxious to see their child's room. It was interesting to see parents carefully taking in the entire room with a glance, noting the toys, books, puzzles, the carpet where their child would listen to stories read by their teacher. Many children recognized friends and began to play with them while other children clung to their parents. Bob knew from experience that the children's behavior was no indication of how the child would react to their first day of school. The child eager to go to school at orientation may be the one who becomes frightened and doesn't want to go on the first day, while the quiet shy child might just march in, take a seat, and be ready to start school.

A few parents, after reading class lists posted on the classroom door, would ask Bob if he could switch their child into a class with his friend. Bob rarely changed children's classes for that reason. He knew it was important for children to form new friendships. And moving one child out of a class meant finding a second child to move into the class to take his place so that the class size would stay the same. Bob did change classes sometimes but usually only if he was asked before the list was printed.

Sometimes a parent had had another child in the teacher's class and felt that the teacher would not be a good fit for her child. Other times, a parent had had another child in the teacher's class and knew it would be a good fit for her younger child. Sometimes a mother wouldn't ask for a particular teacher but asked to keep her child and another child separated because they always fought when they were together.

Many parents would request a teacher like Dorothy, who was loved by so many in the community. Bob was surprised one time when a parent asked that her child not be placed in Dorothy's class. This was a first for Bob. The mother explained that her husband, who had gone to the same school, had been a real troublemaker. She was concerned that an older teacher would remember their father and think his kids would be like him.

The highlight of the day for the children was the ride on the Big Yellow Bus. Children loved this, especially the village kids who would rarely ride the bus. As soon as the three buses were all lined up on the circle, the parents would walk their children out to the circle and wave goodbye as the kids climbed on the buses. The children would peer out the bus windows, and the mothers would wave

## Big Yellow Bus Ride

until the buses were out of sight before going to the cafeteria for a session with Bob. The buses would take the children past their houses and past the familiar spots in the village -- the post office, the library, the grocery store, and the ice cream store -- before eventually taking the children back to school.

Meanwhile in the cafeteria, Bob answered questions from parents. Buses were always a concern. Bob told them to expect the buses to be late the first few days and wanted them to understand that driver were professionals who had extensive driving before being allowed to drive a bus loaded with children. The reason the buses are often late isn't because the driver is learning the route. The real problem is usually that parents and children are learning where the bus stops are and what time to be ready. And children forget things. Often the driver will see a mother running toward the bus, flapping her hands in the air trying to get the driver to wait because her child had left his lunch on the counter.

Since many of the parents in the room had younger children at home, Bob would emphasize that it is never too early to begin reading to your child. Some people consider it a waste of time to read to a baby or toddler that can't ever begin to understand what is being read, but it isn't. This is the first step toward helping children develop a love of reading. Bob also reminded parents that it's never too late to begin reading to children. "They will love it and so will you -- and teachers will thank you."

The fear that their child will make a scene the first day of school is always on the minds of many parents. Once a parent said, "My child is afraid of leaving home and going to school. I know he is going to make a scene when I tell him he has to go to school. I don't know what to do."

Bob assured her that she wasn't alone. He knew this firsthand. And then he told the story about his own son Mike. When the bus arrived on his first day of school, Mike watched his older sisters climb aboard merrily waving good-bye. Then Mike looked at his sisters, at the open bus door, and bolted across the yard and through the large privet hedge. Bob's wife was in hot pursuit. The bus left as Mike shinnied up his favorite climbing tree. No amount of pleading would get him down.

Bob's wife called school, and Bob had to rush home on the first day of school to climb up the tree. Mike was crying. Between sobs he begged, "Dad, please don't make me go to school! I promise, I'll go tomorrow." That is the excuse that many frightened kindergarteners tells their parents. Experience told Bob to ignore his plea.

So there was Bob, crouched precariously near the top of a huge maple tree, trying to pry his five-year-old son from one of the highest branches. His stiff dress shoes were slipping dangerously on the branch and the pocket of his new sports jacket had caught on the bark.

He knew that Mike wasn't scared of heights. What he was scared of was school. It didn't make sense. Bob took his kids to school on weekends, while he caught up on paper work. Mike had been inside the school building many times.

As soon as Bob got Mike down from the tree, he carried him to the car. When they arrived at school, Mike began screaming, "I don't wanna go to school! Don't make me go!" Bob was relieved to hand him over to a teacher. He knew he'd be fine as soon as he got into the classroom – and he was.

The parents laughed when Bob told the story. Bob added, "I treasure that story; however, I'm not certain my son does."

That story gave Bob a chance to ask the parents to share their own stories. He invited them to stop by his office with funny anecdotes or cute stories about their children. "It's a way I can get to know your children better." Bob knew that school intimidated some of the shy parents, but sharing stories gave them a reason to come into the office and talk. Parents quickly learned Bob's reputation as someone who loved a good story, and these stories opened the door to many parents who may otherwise have never approached the principal

And Bob did hear all kinds of stories from parents over the years. One mother told him that her oldest child didn't want to go to school. She kept yelling that she wasn't going to that school.

Her little two-year-old sister yelled, "I'll go for her."

Another child had just transferred from a Catholic school, where the nuns in those days wore full habits. His mother asked him how he liked the new school. "Mom it was great!" he said, "The teachers even wear clothes."

One time a boy broke his arm and Bob sent him a get-well card. He got a phone call the next day from a different mother who said, "My son loves the card you sent, but he doesn't have a broken arm." She told him that the boy across the street, who had the same first name, was the one with the broken arm. Then she laughed, "My son loves the card and asked if he could keep it."

Once at the kindergarten orientation meeting, a parent shared a story with the group about her oldest child's first day of school. She told her daughter that when she went to kindergarten she would learn how to read. Many parents were smiling and nodding their heads. She said, "I couldn't wait for her to come home but instead of giving me a hug and telling me about school, she rushed to her room." A few minutes later her daughter came running down the stairs with her favorite book. She jumped into her mother's lap and proudly opened the book. She turned page after page.

Then she looked up at her mother with great disappointment. With tears welling up in her eyes, she whispered, "Mom, I still can't read."

## Big Yellow Bus Ride

Bob smiled and said, "I love these stories. They help me to better know and understand your children." Then he added, "Please take me up on my offer to visit my office and share your stories. It's a fun way to get to know each other."

Bob saw the buses go by the window and said, "We better get out in front to greet the children so they don't think you abandoned them."

Most of the children were smiling as the busses pulled up to the curb. As soon as the busses stopped, they jumped out of their seats, bounced off the steps of the bus and raced to their parents excitedly telling them about all the things they saw, including seeing their own house. And that was the beginning of another school year.

## About the Authors

*Bob Kinsella*

For twenty years, Bob Kinsella was principal of an elementary school in Minoa, a small village in upstate New York where he still lives. He was an elementary teacher, a high school science teacher, and an associate professor at SUNY College at Cortland, NY in their demonstration school, before his tenure as principal.

Bob received a Ph.D. degree in education from Syracuse University. His interest and enthusiasm for local history has led to numerous articles and essays in regional publications. He is retired and his six children grown, but he continues to be active in the community where some of his grandchildren attended school. He researches and writes for the *Minoa Chronicle*, which is published three times a year and has a readership of about 500.

*Janine DeBaise*

Janine DeBaise, writer and mother of four, has had poetry published in over forty literary magazines, including the *Seattle Review*, the *Minnesota Review*, and *Hawaii Pacific Review*. Her poetry chapbook *Of a Feather* was published by Finishing Line Press in 2003. She has taught various ages and subjects, including fourth grade computer science and seventh grade English.

Janine currently teaches writing and literature at the State University of New York College of Environmental Science and Forestry (SUNY-ESF) in Syracuse, New York. She has given numerous presentations at national conferences on the topics of contemporary nature literature and the pedagogy of teaching composition. She has taught poetry workshops in local elementary schools and has served as poetry judge for the NAACP Afro-academic Culture Technology and Science Olympics.